simply
homemade
food gifts

Meredith. Press
An imprint of Meredith. Books

Meredith® Press
An imprint of Meredith® Books

Simply Homemade Food Gifts

Editors: Jennifer Dorland Darling, Carol Field Dahlstrom
Contributing Editors: Susan M. Banker, Jan Miller, Joyce Trollope
Contributing Writer: Winifred Moranville
Graphic Designer: Marisa Dirks
Copy Chief: Terri Fredrickson
Managers, Book Production: Pam Kvitne, Marjorie J. Schenkelberg
Contributing Copy Editor: Kim Catanzarite
Contributing Proofreaders: Marcia Gilmer, Susan J. Kling, Sherri Schultz
Photographers: Mike Dieter, Pete Krumhardt
Food Stylists: Jill Lust, Dianna Nolin, Charles Worthington
Electronic Production Coordinator: Paula Forest
Editorial and Design Assistants: Judy Bailey, Mary Lee Gavin, Karen Schirm
Test Kitchen Director: Lynn Blanchard
Test Kitchen Product Supervisors: Marilyn Cornelius, Jill Moberly

Meredith® Books
Editor in Chief: James D. Blume
Design Director: Matt Strelecki
Managing Editor: Gregory H. Kayko

Director, Retail Sales and Marketing: Terry Unsworth
Director, Sales, Special Markets: Rita McMullen
Director, Sales, Premiums: Michael A. Peterson
Director, Sales, Retail: Tom Wierzbicki
Director, Book Marketing: Brad Elmitt
Director, Operations: George A. Susral
Director, Production: Douglas M. Johnston

Vice President, General Manager: Jamie L. Martin

Meredith Publishing Group
President, Publishing Group: Stephen M. Lacy
Vice President, Finance and Administration: Max Runciman

Meredith Corporation
Chairman and Chief Executive Officer: William T. Kerr

Chairman of the Executive Committee: E. T. Meredith III

This seal assures you that
every recipe in *Simply Homemade
Food Gifts* has been tested in the
Better Homes and Gardens®
Test Kitchen. This means that each
recipe is practical and reliable,
and meets high standards
of taste appeal.

All of us at Meredith® Books are dedicated to providing you with the information and ideas you need to create delicious foods and beautiful and useful projects. We welcome your comments and suggestions. Write to us at: Meredith Books, Cookbook Editorial Department, 1716 Locust St., Des Moines, IA 50309-3023.

Permission to photocopy Preparation Directions on pages 15, 19, 27, 59, 65, 73, 77, 95, 101, 105, 129, 167, 201, and 207 for personal gift-giving is granted by Meredith Books.

If you would like to purchase any of our books, check wherever quality books are sold. Visit us at meredithbooks.com
Pictured on front cover: Viennese Coffee Balls (see recipe, page 75)
Cover photograph: Pete Krumhardt

giving thanks 6
More than a dozen thoughtful ways to say thank you, from a box of edible hugs and kisses to a fruit-topped jar of topping.

bright birthday wishes 38
Whether they're wild and crazy or charmingly old-fashioned, your unique friends deserve unique birthday gifts, and that's just what you'll find here.

cherished gifts for all seasons 80
From a surefire way to steal someone's heart on Valentine's Day to heartwarming gifts for December nights, here are meaningful ways to mark seasonal occasions throughout the year.

merry gifts for christmas 130
Good things come in all sorts of packages when you tuck holiday sweets, nibbles, mixes, and more goodies inside beautifully decorated boxes and other festive containers.

between friends & neighbors 176
Call on these condiments, quick breads, luscious spreads, and other tasty ideas to welcome a new neighbor, say goodbye to an old friend, and mark heartfelt moments of friendship and sharing.

meaningful gifts from the heart and hearth

Some people touch our lives in special ways. You know who they are. The assistant who saved the day (again!) … your friend who always says just what you need to hear … the teacher who stayed late to explain the math problem one more time … the neighbor who's allergic to cats but keeps an eye out for yours all the same.

Sometimes finding the perfect gift for such people calls for more than a trip to the mall. After all, don't one-of-a-kind people deserve one-of-a-kind gifts? We think so.

Peruse the pages of this book, and you'll find just the right gift for anyone who has touched your life. Inside, there are more than 100 beautifully packaged, memorable food gift ideas, for every reason and season. Each pleases the palate and touches the heart in the way only homemade food gifts can.

Yes, you can do it! We've combined our talents as a veteran food editor and an experienced crafts editor to make sure every project is simple and doable, no matter what your level of expertise. And every recipe has been tested to perfection in the Better Homes and Gardens® Test Kitchen. We know that when you take time from your busy schedule to create a homemade food gift, you want results you'll be proud to share.

So next time you're looking for that perfect gift for someone close to your heart, browse through this book of projects and take your pick. We're sure you'll love the results—not only the goodies themselves, but the smiles and cheer your heartfelt gift will bring.

Jennifer Dorland Darling

Jennifer Dorland Darling

Carol Field Dahlstrom

Carol Field Dahlstrom

before you begin

be sure to read these tips thoroughly. They provide information you need to know concerning all the projects in this book.

FINDING ITEMS YOU NEED:

new items, such as cheese trays, bottles, cake plates, and sugar bowls, can be purchased inexpensively at discount or housewares stores. Find vintage and collectible items at flea markets, antiques stores, garage sales, and thrift shops. For crafting materials, look in crafts stores; for harder-to-find items, check out the source list on page 215.

WHEN MAKING THE GIFT:

read the recipe and craft instructions before you begin. Make sure you have the utensils, food, and crafting materials at hand before you start. Items you need are listed to the right of the craft instructions, making it easy for you to gather the materials beforehand.

choose the proper container: Make sure any container you use to store or package food is food safe.

use proper crafting materials: When possible, use crafting materials that are nontoxic and food safe. When using non-food-safe materials, such as glitter, paints, glues, inks, etc., line the container and cover the food with plastic wrap, waxed paper, parchment paper, tissue paper, or foil to keep the food from coming into direct contact with these materials.

wash and dry all containers thoroughly before using.

WHEN GIVING THE GIFT:

give storage instructions too. Each recipe tells you how to store the food—whether in the freezer, refrigerator, or at room temperature, whether in containers or wrapped in plastic wrap, etc. Recipes also indicate how long the food can be stored. Keep in mind that the container you use to present the gift may not be the proper container for storing the gift. Therefore, be sure to pass along the storage instructions to the recipient. That

way, any food not consumed right away can be safely stored. How long the food can be stored also depends on how long you've stored the food gift in your own home since preparing it. Take this into consideration when sharing storage instructions.

offer serving suggestions: Recipes for foods such as spreads, dips, rubs, condiments, and flavored vinegars often come with serving instructions and suggestions. These appear in the method or in the note that precedes the method. Pass along these points with the gift so the recipient knows how to serve and enjoy the food.

include preparation directions: For foods that require reheating or other specific instructions, we've included boxes that list Preparation Directions. Include these with the gift. Photocopy the box and paste it onto the gift tag, or copy the instructions onto a gift card.

TOTING THE GIFT:

the packaging for some gifts, such as the Hugs and Kisses Spritz, page 21, works well for both presenting and toting the gift. However, other gifts require a little ingenuity when it comes to transporting them to their destinations. Here are a few ideas:

gifts presented on plates or trays, such as the Lemon Cupcakes, page 13, usually can be toted as shown; simply cover with plastic wrap before setting out. Once the gift is covered, you can also bundle it in cellophane.

for gifts with multiple components, such as the Chai, page 19, use a gift box or bag in which to tote all components of the gift.

for other gifts, such as the Cheddar Crackers, page 11, it makes sense to carry the food in a different container than the crafted container, then assemble the presentation once you've arrived at your destination.

Fermented Fruit Topping,
page 29

giving thanks

giving thanks giving thanks giving thanks gi

tempting trayful

Easy-to-make chocolate treats nestled inside an antique butter dish say thanks in a sweet and simple way.

TO MAKE THE RECIPE...

simple fudge tarts

Nonstick cooking spray

½ of an 18-ounce roll refrigerated peanut butter cookie dough

½ cup semisweet chocolate pieces

¼ cup sweetened condensed milk

Novice cooks (and experienced cooks short on time), take note: Thanks to a shortcut cookie-dough crust, just three ingredients add up to chocolaty rich tartlets that are pure pleasure to receive!

1 Lightly coat twenty-four 1¾-inch muffin cups with nonstick cooking spray or line with paper or foil bake cups; set aside.

2 For tart shells, cut cookie dough into 6 equal pieces. Cut each piece into 4 equal slices. Place each slice of dough in a prepared cup.

3 Bake in a 350° oven for 9 minutes or until edges are light brown and dough is slightly firm but not set. Remove tart shells from oven. Gently press a shallow indentation in each tart shell with the back of a round ½-teaspoon measuring spoon. Bake 2 minutes more or until the edges of tart shells are firm and light golden brown. Let tart shells cool in cups on a wire rack for 15 minutes. Carefully remove tart shells from cups. Cool completely on wire racks.

4 For filling, in a small saucepan combine chocolate pieces and sweetened condensed milk. Cook and stir over medium heat until chocolate is melted. Spoon a slightly rounded teaspoon of filling into each cooled tart shell. (Or, if desired, spoon the slightly cooled melted chocolate mixture into a small self-sealing plastic bag. Cut off one corner of the bag and pipe fudge mixture into each tart shell.) Cool completely, allowing filling to set. Store in a tightly covered container at room temperature for up to 3 days or in the freezer for up to 1 month. Makes 24 tarts.

TO PRESENT THIS GIFT... Arrange a single layer of tarts in the dish. Tie a ribbon around the dish, making a bow with the ends. Trim the ribbon ends, if desired.

also try this...

Place the tarts in decorative vintage glassware such as small relish trays, saucers, or casseroles.

To present this gift you will need:
Antique clear glass butter dish
Ribbon
Scissors

folded fun

This clever cracker holder harkens back to the folded paper toys of childhood, a perfect way to express gratitude to a longtime friend.

cheddar crackers

Make the dough for these crisp appetizer tidbits in advance and freeze up to 6 months. Thaw in the refrigerator, then simply slice, bake, and cool before packing the crackers into the paper holders.

2 cups shredded sharp cheddar cheese (8 ounces)
$\frac{1}{2}$ cup butter
1$\frac{1}{2}$ cups all-purpose flour
$\frac{1}{4}$ to $\frac{1}{2}$ teaspoon salt
$\frac{1}{4}$ teaspoon ground red pepper

1 In a large mixing bowl combine shredded cheese and butter; bring to room temperature (about 1 hour).

2 Beat with an electric mixer until combined. Stir in flour, salt, and red pepper. Divide the dough in half. Shape dough into two 7-inch logs. Wrap and chill logs for at least 1 hour.

3 Using a knife or a crinkle cutter, cut the cheese logs into $\frac{1}{4}$-inch slices. Place slices on ungreased baking sheets. Bake in a 350° oven for 15 minutes. Cool on a wire rack. Store in a tightly covered container in the refrigerator for up to 1 week or in the freezer for up to 3 months. Makes about 54 crackers.

TO PRESENT THIS GIFT... Cut the paper into a 12-inch square. The larger the square, the larger the cracker holder. Pinpoint the center of the square by prefolding. To do this, bring two opposite sides together to fold the square in half. Unfold the paper and bring the remaining two opposite sides together and fold the paper in half again. Unfold the paper and bring the four corners to the center of the square. Flip this smaller square over and fold all four corners into the center. Fold this even smaller square in half and insert your thumb and forefinger into each of the four outer pockets. Bring your fingertips together to shape the container, then remove them. Invert container to expose pockets, right side up. Your four-pocketed container is ready to fill.

also try this...

Choose decorative papers appropriate for the season or celebration to give Cheddar Crackers year-round.

To present this gift you will need:
Decorative paper in desired color
Scissors
Ruler

the sweetest little
baby cakes

Got a whole family to thank? **Give each family member a cake of their own. Present them on a dainty cut-glass plate that will be cherished long after the goodies are gone.**

lemon cupcakes

Some cakes dry quickly, and therefore don't make suitable gifts. Not these! A penetrating glaze of fresh lemon juice and sugar imbues the mini-cakes with a moistness that lasts for days.

2	cups all-purpose flour
2½	teaspoons baking powder
¼	teaspoon salt
⅔	cup shortening
1	cup sugar
3	eggs
⅔	cup milk
1	tablespoon finely shredded lemon peel
⅔	cup sugar
⅓	cup lemon juice
	Lemon peel curls (optional)
	Fresh lemon balm leaves (optional)

1 Grease and lightly flour twenty to twenty-four 2½-inch muffin cups. Combine flour, baking powder, and salt; set aside.

2 In a large mixing bowl beat shortening with an electric mixer on medium to high speed for 30 seconds. Add the 1 cup sugar and beat until combined. Add eggs, one at a time, beating well after each addition. Alternately add flour mixture and milk, beating on low to medium speed after each addition just until combined. Stir in the 1 tablespoon lemon peel. Spoon batter into prepared muffin cups. (Fill any empty, greased muffin cups with water to avoid damaging pan.)

3 Bake in a 350° oven for 20 to 25 minutes or until a wooden toothpick inserted in centers comes out clean. Cool in pans on wire racks for 5 minutes. Remove from pans. Place cupcakes upside down on wire racks set over waxed paper.

4 In a small mixing bowl stir together the ⅔ cup sugar and the lemon juice. Brush sugar mixture over warm cupcakes until all is absorbed. Cool completely. Cover and store in the refrigerator for up to 5 days or in an airtight container in the freezer for up to 2 months. Before serving, garnish with lemon peel curls and lemon balm leaves, if desired. Makes 20 to 24 cupcakes.

Place a serving plate on the watercolor paper and trace around it. Cut out the shape 1 inch smaller than the drawn line. Mix food coloring with water to desired color. "Paint" a design on the paper as desired. Let dry. Center the paper on the plate and arrange the cupcakes on top.

also try this...

Use colored cellophane, found at paper goods stores, to cut and use as a plate liner.

To present this gift you will need:
Clear glass serving plate
Watercolor paper
Pencil
Scissors
Food coloring
Clean paintbrushes

blueberry
bounty

Vintage handkerchiefs add old-fashioned warmth to this long-handled basket that bears both a jar of scone mix and a sampling fresh from the oven.

TO MAKE THE RECIPE...

blueberry tea scone mix

⅓ cup Vanilla Sugar (see recipe below)
2 cups all-purpose flour
¼ cup nonfat dry milk powder
2 teaspoons baking powder
1 teaspoon dried lemon peel
¼ teaspoon salt
⅓ cup shortening that does not require refrigeration
1 cup dried blueberries

The Vanilla Sugar recipe, below, makes a fine gift on its own. Present it in a ribbon-wrapped jar and suggest sprinkling over baked goods or stirring into coffee drinks.

1 Prepare Vanilla Sugar. In a large mixing bowl stir together the flour, the ⅓ cup Vanilla Sugar, milk powder, baking powder, lemon peel, and salt. Using a pastry blender, cut in shortening until mixture resembles coarse crumbs. Stir in blueberries.

2 Layer flour mixture and blueberries in a 1-quart jar, starting with the flour mixture. Tap jar gently on the counter to settle contents. Add additional dried blueberries to fill small gaps, if necessary. Cover and store mix in refrigerator for up to 6 weeks or in freezer for up to 6 months. Makes 1 jar mix.

Vanilla Sugar: Fill a 1-quart jar with 4 cups sugar. Cut a vanilla bean in half lengthwise and insert both halves into sugar. Secure lid and store in a cool, dry place for several weeks before using. Will keep indefinitely.

TO PRESENT THIS GIFT...

Arrange hankies in the basket with some of the edges folded over the side of the basket. Tie a generous ribbon bow around the jar containing the prepared scone mix. Trim the ribbon ends, if necessary. Place the jar in the basket. Arrange ready-to-eat scones around the jar. Include preparation directions, below, with gift.

also try this...
Use clean fabric scraps as an alternative to the handkerchiefs.

To present this gift you will need:
Clean new or vintage handkerchiefs
Basket
Ribbon
Scissors

PREPARATION DIRECTIONS

blueberry tea scones

1 egg, beaten
¼ cup water
Milk (optional)
Coarse sugar (optional)

1 Place contents of the jar in a large mixing bowl. Add egg and water; stir just until moistened. Turn dough out onto a lightly floured surface and quickly knead by folding and gently pressing for 12 to 15 strokes or until nearly smooth.

2 Pat dough into an 8-inch circle. Cut into 10 wedges, dipping knife into flour between cuts. Place wedges 1 inch apart on an ungreased baking sheet. Brush tops with milk and sprinkle with coarse sugar, if desired.

3 Bake in a 400° oven for 12 to 15 minutes or until golden. Transfer to a wire rack to cool slightly. Serve warm. Makes 10 scones.

spreadable
cheer

A terra-cotta saucer complements this richly colored spread. Handmade with care, the clay-crafted knife makes a marvelous keepsake.

½ cup chopped onion
2 tablespoons cooking oil
1 cup raisins
1 cup dry red wine
½ cup snipped, oil-packed dried tomatoes, drained
¼ teaspoon ground cloves

raisin-spice spread

Be sure to tell the recipient that this fruit-and-spice (and everything nice) spread makes a tasty treat partnered with melba rounds, bagel chips, or toast.

1 In a large skillet cook onion in hot oil over medium heat until tender. Add raisins, wine, drained tomatoes, and cloves. Bring to boiling; reduce heat. Simmer, uncovered, until liquid is reduced to about 2 tablespoons and raisins are soft.

2 Transfer mixture to a food processor bowl and process until coarsely chopped. Transfer to glass storage container. Cover and store in the refrigerator for up to 2 weeks. To serve, heat the spread or serve it chilled as a spread for bread, toast, melba rounds, bagel chips, or crackers. Makes about 1 cup spread.

TO PRESENT THIS GIFT... Roll out two coils of clay in different colors. Place coils side by side. Wrap the coils in decorative fashion around the knife handle. Bake in a glass baking dish in the oven according to the clay manufacturer's instructions. Let cool. Place shredded paper in the bottom of the terra-cotta saucer. Fill the glass bowl with Raisin-Spice Spread and place on top of the shredded paper. Place knife on top.

also try this...

Embellish the terra-cotta saucer in a similar manner using decorative clay shapes such as zigzags or circles.

To present this gift you will need:
Oven-bake clay in desired colors
Spreader knife with a plain handle
Glass baking dish
Shredded crinkle paper
Terra-cotta flowerpot saucer
Small glass bowl

teatime twist

CHAI TEA

Get in on the chai craze and get your friends in on it too! Share the passion for this new beverage by presenting the decoratively wrapped mix with a teapot or another teatime collectible.

TO MAKE THE RECIPE...

chai

1¼ cups nonfat dry milk powder
¼ cup black tea leaves
12 cardamom pods
4 2-inch pieces stick cinnamon
2 teaspoons dried lemon peel

This recipe is for 2 bags of Chai mix, but if you prefer to make one large gift, you can layer all the mix in one larger cellophane bag or one 12-ounce jar or bottle. Simply revise the preparation directions, below, instructing the recipient to mix the jar's contents with 8 cups of water for 8 servings.

1 In two clean cellophane bags or two 6-ounce jars or bottles, layer all ingredients. Seal bag or cover jar and store in a cool, dry place for up to 3 months. Makes 2 bags mix.

TO PRESENT THIS GIFT...

Fill the cellophane bag with prepared Chai mix as directed in recipe; tie with a loose ribbon bow. Trim the ribbon ends, if desired. Tie two cinnamon sticks together with a ribbon bow; tuck into larger bow.

For the tag, cut three slightly different-size shapes from colored papers. Cut with decorative scissors, if desired. Glue one on top of the other. Let the glue dry. Punch a hole in one corner. Thread cord through hole. Include preparation directions, below, with gift.

also try this...

Personalize a plain glass teapot by painting an initial on one side using paints specifically made for glass. Let the paint dry. Bake the painted glassware in the oven if instructed by the paint manufacturer. Let cool.

To present this gift you will need:
Cellophane bag
18-inch length of 1-inch-wide ribbon
Scissors
2 cinnamon sticks
Ribbon
Colored paper in 3 colors
Decorative scissors (optional)
Thick white crafts glue
Paper punch
Cord
Teapot

PREPARATION DIRECTIONS

chai

4 cups water
Honey

In a large saucepan combine contents of bag with the water. Bring to boiling; remove from heat. Cover and let stand for 5 minutes. Strain through a wire sieve lined with 100-percent-cotton cheesecloth or a clean paper coffee filter. To serve, add honey to sweeten to taste. Makes 4 1-cup servings.

a box of hugs and kisses

Tins of butter cookies have long been a cherished gift-giving tradition. Here the idea gets personal, conveying your heartfelt thanks with unmistakable affection.

TO MAKE THE RECIPE...

hugs and kisses spritz

1½ cups butter
1 cup granulated sugar
1 teaspoon baking powder
1 egg
1 teaspoon vanilla
¼ teaspoon almond extract (optional)
3½ cups all-purpose flour
Coarse or colored sugar (optional)

Remember—it's best to use butter when it comes to these all-time favorite cookies. Margarine just won't offer the hallmark buttery flavor so loved in the classic.

1 In a large mixing bowl beat butter with an electric mixer on medium to high speed for 30 seconds. Add granulated sugar and baking powder. Beat until combined, scraping bowl. Beat in egg, vanilla, and, if desired, almond extract until combined. Beat in as much of the flour as you can with the mixer. Stir in any remaining flour with a wooden spoon.

2 Force unchilled dough through a cookie press into Xs and Os onto an ungreased cookie sheet. Sprinkle lightly with coarse or colored sugar, if desired.

3 Bake in a 375° oven for 8 to 10 minutes or until edges are firm but not brown. Transfer cookies to a wire rack to cool. Store in a tightly covered container at room temperature for up to 3 days or in the freezer for up to 6 months. Makes about 84 cookies.

TO PRESENT THIS GIFT... In a well-ventilated work area, spray-paint the lid and base of tin gold. Let dry. Using fabric paints, draw Xs and Os on top of the lid and on the sides of the tin. Let the paint dry. Line box and cover cookies with parchment paper, waxed paper, or plastic wrap to protect food from coming into contact with spray-painted surfaces. Wrap box with ribbon; tie ribbon into a bow.

For the tag, cut two slightly different-size squares from gold and silver papers. Cut rounded corners on each of the squares. Glue the smaller square on top of the larger one. Let dry. Glue small gold jewels in each corner. Let dry. Punch a hole near the edge. Thread a ribbon through the hole to attach to the package.

also try this...
Use fabric paints to write a personalized message on the ribbon.

To present this gift you will need:
Square food tin
Gold spray paint
Fabric paints in copper and glitter silver
Parchment paper, waxed paper, or plastic wrap
Ribbon
Scissors
Gold and silver papers
Thick white crafts glue
Small gold jewels
Paper punch
Narrow ribbon

cheese to please

A mismatched (but well-chosen) dish-and-saucer duo make
a fitting old-world vessel for this handcrafted cheese.

fresh yogurt cheese

- 1 16-ounce carton plain yogurt or plain goat's milk yogurt*
- 2 teaspoons finely snipped fresh herbs, such as basil, thyme, oregano, marjoram, chervil, rosemary, or parsley; or ½ teaspoon ground spice, such as black pepper, white pepper, red pepper, coriander, or chili powder (optional)

Giving a gift of homemade cheese may sound like a complicated endeavor, but it's not. Simply start with yogurt, then separate the curds (the cheese) from the whey (the liquid). The result: an impressive, pleasingly tangy spread for crackers or bread.

1 Line a yogurt strainer, sieve, or small colander with three layers of 100-percent-cotton cheesecloth or a clean paper coffee filter. Suspend lined strainer, sieve, or colander over a bowl.

2 Spoon in yogurt. Cover with plastic wrap. Refrigerate for at least 24 hours. Remove from refrigerator. Discard liquid.

3 Transfer cheese to a bowl. Stir herbs or spices into the cheese, if desired. Cover and store in refrigerator for up to 1 week. Makes ¾ to 1 cup cheese.

*Note: Use a brand of yogurt that contains no gums, gelatin, or fillers. These ingredients may prevent the whey from separating from the curd to make cheese.

Place the prepared yogurt cheese in the pedestal dish and garnish the top with fresh herb sprigs. Place the dish on a saucer. Place a gold spoon on the saucer to use as a server.

For the tag, cut a small piece of light-colored paper into a pie-piece shape. Cut off the point. Glue on top of a yellow paper doily. Let glue dry. Trim the doily as shown. Use a paper punch to make a hole at the top. Thread the hole with ribbon. Tie the tag around the pedestal dish. Offer purchased crackers alongside the gift, if desired.

also try this...

You can use other mismatched vintage glassware pieces, such as sugar bowls, creamers, cups, or dessert bowls.

To present this gift you will need:
Small pedestal dish
Fresh herb sprigs
Elegant teacup saucer
Gold spoon
Scissors
Light-colored paper
Glue stick
Yellow paper doily
Paper punch
Narrow ribbon
Purchased crackers (optional)

summer-fresh
thank-you

The next time a green-thumbed friend shares a bumper crop of fresh vegetables, return the favor in the form of this raffia-wrapped, summery dip.

- 3 cups finely chopped tomato
- 1 cup finely chopped cucumber
- ½ cup finely chopped red onion
- ½ cup finely chopped sweet yellow pepper
- ¼ cup snipped fresh cilantro
- 1 tablespoon red wine vinegar
- 2 teaspoons olive oil
- ½ teaspoon salt
- ¼ teaspoon sugar
- 1 to 2 small fresh serrano peppers, seeded and finely chopped*
- 2 cloves garlic, minced

gazpacho salsa

When you use fresh, locally grown ingredients, this dip will really pop with the flavors and colors of summer. Inspired by a well-known Andalusian soup, it's so good the recipient will be tempted to eat it with a spoon, though we suggest tortilla chips!

1 In a bowl combine tomato, cucumber, onion, sweet pepper, cilantro, vinegar, oil, salt, sugar, serrano peppers, and garlic. Cover and chill for at least 1 hour before serving. Store in the refrigerator for up to 2 days. Makes about 4 cups salsa.

*Note: Hot peppers contain volatile oils that can burn eyes, lips, and sensitive skin. Wear plastic gloves while working with peppers, and be sure to wash your hands thoroughly afterward.

Measure the neck of the container. Cut several strands of green raffia 16 inches longer than measurement. Tie the raffia around the neck of the glass container. Tie the raffia ends into a bow, tucking a fresh hot pepper into bow. Trim ends, if desired.

For the tag, use pinking shears to cut a small square from the red paper and a slightly smaller square from the green paper. Center and glue the green square on top of the red one. Let glue dry. Punch a hole in one corner and thread through a strand or two of raffia.

also try this...

Use jute to tie around the neck of the container. For added color, thread wood beads on the jute ends and knot to secure.

To present this gift you will need:
Tape measure
Glass container with glass lid
Scissors
Green raffia
Fresh hot chile pepper (see note, above)
Pinking shears
Decorative papers in red and green
Thick white crafts glue
Paper punch

honey buns

Friends and family will love **fresh-from-the-oven Cinnamon Buns.** A pan with a decorative handle might also inspire their own baked creations.

cinnamon buns

- 1   16-ounce loaf frozen sweet roll dough
- 6   tablespoons butter
- 3   cups sifted powdered sugar
- 2   teaspoons vanilla
- 4 to 6 teaspoons milk
- 1   teaspoon ground cinnamon
- ½   cup miniature semisweet chocolate pieces and/or chopped nuts
  Small multicolored decorative candies (optional)

It's up to you—you can present these all-time favorite breakfast rolls frosted and still slightly warm from the oven for immediate enjoyment. Or wrap and chill the frosting and rolls separately, attaching the preparation instructions alongside the gift.

1 Thaw dough as directed on package. Grease eighteen 2½-inch muffin cups or two 8×1½-inch round baking pans; set aside.

2 In a medium saucepan heat butter over low heat until melted. Continue heating until butter turns a delicate brown. Remove from heat; pour into a small bowl. Stir in powdered sugar, vanilla, and enough milk to make spreading consistency. Remove ⅓ cup of the mixture; to this ⅓ cup mixture, stir in cinnamon to make filling. Cover and set aside. Cover remaining plain mixture to use as frosting and set aside.

3 Turn dough out onto a lightly floured surface. Roll dough into a 12×8-inch rectangle. Spread the filling evenly over dough to within ½ inch of edges. Sprinkle with chocolate pieces and/or nuts, if desired. Roll up into a spiral, starting from a long side. Moisten edge and pinch seam to seal. Slice roll into 18 equal

pieces. (Or, for larger rolls, cut dough into 12 rolls and bake in muffin pans or one greased 9×1½-inch round baking pan.) Place slices, cut sides down, in prepared muffin cups or baking pans. Cover; let rise in a warm place until nearly double (45 to 60 minutes). Bake in a 350° oven for 15 to 18 minutes or until golden brown.

4 To present as a gift immediately, remove from pans. Cool slightly on wire rack. If necessary, add a small amount of additional milk to frosting to make spreading consistency. Spread frosting on top of rolls. Sprinkle with candies, if desired.

5 To give at a later date, remove rolls from pan. Cool unfrosted rolls. Wrap in decorative plastic wrap or place in an airtight container. Package frosting separately. (Rolls and frosting may be frozen for up to 1 month. Thaw in refrigerator before giving.) Attach preparation instructions with gift. Makes 12 to 18 rolls.

Cut three 18-inch lengths from each color of wire. With the wire ends even, wrap a rubber band tightly around the wires, approximately 3 inches from one end. Separate the wires, grouping colors together. Braid the wires together, leaving 3 inches at the end unbraided. Slip each group of wires through the tops of the paper holders. Knot each group of wires at the ends to secure. Return baked rolls to the clean pan. Clip the paper holders over the pan edge to create a handle. Form the wires into an arch. Include preparation instructions, right, with gift.

also try this...

Use this quick-to-make handle on bowls or baskets that do not have handles.

To present this gift you will need:
- Wire cutters
- Plastic-coated wire in three desired colors
- Small rubber band
- Pinch-style paper holders (binder clips)
- Clean pan

PREPARATION DIRECTIONS
Wrap unfrosted rolls in foil. Heat in a 300° oven for 15 to 20 minutes or until warm. Stir frosting to soften, adding a little milk, if necessary. Spread frosting over rolls.

fruit-topped
rumtopf

It's hard to say which is prettier: the fruit-topped jar or the dessert sauce inside. Combined, they make a memorable gift.

fermented fruit topping

1½ cups packed brown sugar
1 cup water
4 large pears, cored and cut up
4 medium nectarines or peeled peaches, pitted and sliced; or one 16-ounce package frozen unsweetened peach slices, thawed
2 cups seedless red grapes, halved (optional)
1 medium pineapple, peeled, cored, and cut up
2½ to 3 cups rum

Here's a fresh, updated version of fermented fruit. It's based on a German and Austrian specialty known as "rumtopf," which means "rum pot." In any language, it's wonderful on pound cake or ice cream.

1 In a saucepan combine brown sugar and water. Cook and stir over medium-low heat until sugar is dissolved; cool. In a 4-quart, tall, nonmetal crock or jar combine fruit; pour in syrup mixture.

2 Add enough rum to cover the fruit; stir gently to combine. Store, covered, in a cool place overnight. Place in the refrigerator and store, covered, for up to 4 months, stirring occasionally, using portions as desired.* Let fruit stand at room temperature 30 minutes before serving. Makes about 3 quarts mixture.

*Note: To replenish Fermented Fruit Topping, add 2 cups chopped fruit and ½ cup packed brown sugar to replace every 2 cups of fruit and syrup removed (the top layer of fruit may darken during storage). Store in the refrigerator.

Glue one end of the cord to the center of the jar lid. Wind the cord around to the outer rim, being careful not to overlap onto the ring of the lid. Glue in place. Cut off the excess cord. Tie the remaining cord around the neck of the jar. Glue leaves from artificial fruit to the ends of the cord. Arrange and glue the fruit on top of the cord-covered lid. Place the fruit in the center so the ring of the lid can be removed. Let the glue dry.

also try this...

Make your own artificial fruit with polymer clay. Use snippets of twigs for stems.

To present this gift you will need:
Silicon glue
1 yard of ivory satin cord
Jar, of desired size, with ring lid
Artificial fruit

the envelope, please!

Use pressed-petal paper **to create envelopes that lend beauty and individuality to gifts of home-baked goodness.**

walnut-crowned banana muffins

½ cup finely chopped walnuts and/or almonds

2 tablespoons granulated sugar

¼ teaspoon ground cinnamon

2 cups all-purpose flour

½ cup packed brown sugar

2 teaspoons baking powder

½ teaspoon baking soda

½ teaspoon ground cinnamon

¼ teaspoon salt

1 egg, beaten

2 medium ripe bananas, mashed (about ⅔ cup)

⅔ cup buttermilk

¼ cup butter or margarine, melted

After adding the banana mixture to the flour mixture, be sure not to overmix the batter. Stir it just until moistened; overmixing can cause peaks, tunnels, and a tough texture.

1 Grease twelve 2½-inch muffin cups or line with paper bake cups; set aside. For nut topping, in a small mixing bowl stir together the nuts, granulated sugar, and the ¼ teaspoon ground cinnamon. Set aside.

2 In a large mixing bowl stir together the flour, brown sugar, baking powder, baking soda, the ½ teaspoon cinnamon, and the salt. In a medium mixing bowl stir together the egg, banana, buttermilk, and melted butter. Add banana mixture all at once to the flour mixture. Stir just until moistened (batter should be lumpy). Spoon batter into prepared muffin cups, filling each almost full. Sprinkle about 2 teaspoons of the nut topping on top of each muffin.

3 Bake in a 400° oven about 20 minutes or until a wooden toothpick inserted in centers comes out clean. Cool 5 minutes in muffin cups. Remove from muffin cups and cool completely on a wire rack. Place in an airtight container or bag. Seal and store at room temperature for up to 3 days. To reheat muffins before serving, wrap them in foil. Reheat in a 300° oven for 10 to 12 minutes. Makes 12 muffins.

Cut a 10×15-inch rectangle and a 3×22-inch strip from decorative paper. Make two folds in the rectangle, one at 6 inches and another at 9 inches. Make two crosswise folds in the strip, one at 6 inches and another at 16 inches. Lay the right (printed) side of the rectangle against your work surface. Apply glue to the center section of the rectangle. Press the center of the strip into the glue right (printed) side down. The extending sides of the strip will fold up to make the side of the envelope. Let the glue dry. Bring the two wide flaps of the rectangle up, aligning edges. Punch two sets of matching holes 1 inch from the top edge and 3 inches in from each side. Bring the narrow side strip ends up. With right (printed) sides together, pinch each strip in half at the top. Tuck the strip ends between the wide flaps and secure with tape, if necessary. Line envelopes with parchment or waxed paper and fill with muffins. String a ribbon through the punched holes and tie the ends together. Push the stems of two leaves into the center of the bow, if desired. Include reheating instructions (in step 3 of recipe, above) with gift.

also try this...

For a natural spin, use clean brown paper to make the envelopes and raffia for the bow.

To present this gift you will need:

Scissors
Ruler
Purchased paper with pressed flowers and leaves
Thick white crafts glue
Paper punch
1 yard of ribbon
Tape, optional
Parchment paper or waxed paper
2 leaves (optional)

congenial
conserves

Sweet conserves say thanks and more when presented on a serving coaster decorated with little wooden apples and easy painting tricks.

TO MAKE THE RECIPE...

apple-nutmeg conserve

- 5 cups chopped, peeled apples
- 1 cup water
- ⅓ cup lemon juice
- 1 1¾-ounce package regular powdered fruit pectin
- 4 cups sugar
- 1 cup golden raisins
- ½ teaspoon ground nutmeg

When presenting this apple-orchard-inspired gift, tell the recipient that it makes a marvelous spread on pita bread wedges arranged around a bowl of cheese cubes.

1 In a 6- or 8-quart Dutch oven or kettle combine the chopped apples, water, and lemon juice. Bring to boiling; reduce heat. Cover and simmer for 10 minutes.

2 Stir in powdered pectin and bring to a full rolling boil, stirring constantly. Stir in sugar and raisins. Return to a full rolling boil. Boil hard for 1 minute, stirring constantly. Remove from heat; stir in nutmeg.

3 Immediately ladle into hot, sterilized half-pint canning jars, leaving ¼-inch headspace. Wipe jar rims and adjust lids. Process the filled jars in a boiling-water canner for 5 minutes (start timing when water begins to boil). Remove jars from canner; cool on racks. Makes 6 half-pints conserve.

TO PRESENT THIS GIFT... Paint the wood circle dark red. Let the paint dry. Paint on a thick coat of crackling medium. Let it dry. Paint ivory over the crackling medium, being careful not to repaint any strokes. The paint will crackle as it dries. When dry, sand edges for a worn appearance. Glue a ring of apples, large enough to encircle the jar of conserves, around the outer edge of the wood circle. Let the glue dry. Place conserve jar in circle of apples. Tie a ribbon around the top of the jar.

also try this...

Inexpensive wood coasters also work well for the base of this holder.

To present this gift you will need:
4½-inch purchased wood circle
Acrylic paints in dark red and ivory
Paintbrush
Crackling medium
Sandpaper
Thick white crafts glue
20×20-mm red wood apples
Ribbon in desired color

raspberry revel

The raspberries on top of the jar and the chocolate-colored drippings on the box are subtle yet enticing clues to what's inside!

TO MAKE THE RECIPE...

raspberry-fudge sauce

- ¾ cup unsweetened cocoa powder
- ⅔ cup granulated sugar
- ⅔ cup packed brown sugar
- 1 cup whipping cream
- ⅓ cup butter
- 3 ounces bittersweet or semisweet chocolate, finely chopped
- 3 tablespoons raspberry liqueur

Raspberry and chocolate are a match made in confection heaven. Can you think of a sweeter way to express your gratitude?

1 In a small mixing bowl stir together the cocoa powder, granulated sugar, and brown sugar. Set aside.

2 In a heavy medium saucepan heat whipping cream and butter over low heat until butter is melted, stirring constantly. Cook and stir over medium heat about 3 minutes or until mixture bubbles around edges. Add sugar mixture. Cook, stirring constantly, for 1 to 2 minutes more or until sugar is dissolved and mixture is smooth and thickened. Remove from heat.

3 Stir chocolate and raspberry liqueur into fudge mixture until chocolate is melted. Pour sauce into clean, dry half-pint jars. Seal with a lid. Store in the refrigerator for up to 1 week. Heat sauce before serving over sundaes, cakes, or other desserts. Makes 3 half-pint jars sauce.

TO PRESENT THIS GIFT...

Paint the box with cream-colored paint. Let dry. Use a paint pen to paint around the top edge of the box, adding drips to look like chocolate. In a well-ventilated work area, spray-paint the canning ring from the jar lid red, if desired. Let dry. Use the lid to trace a circle on the cream-colored paper. Cut out. Insert the paper circle under the ring on the jar lid. Hot-glue a small cluster of artificial raspberries onto the paper circle. Let dry. (If using spray paint, cover sauce jar with a small piece of plastic wrap before twisting on the lid to protect food from touching spray paint.) Tie a ribbon bow to the box handle. Place the jar in the box.

also try this...

If the wood box does not have a cutout, write "Raspberry-Fudge Sauce" on the front using a paint pen.

To present this gift you will need:
Purchased small wood box with a handle and with desired cutout
Cream-colored acrylic paint
Paintbrush
Chocolate-brown-colored paint pen
Canning jar
Red spray paint (optional)
Cream-colored paper
Hot-glue gun and hot-glue sticks
Artificial raspberries with leaves
Plastic wrap
Ribbon

movie-night delight

Spice up video night at home for someone special with a bottle of zippy popcorn mix tucked inside a pretty napkin.

pesto popcorn seasoning mix

3 tablespoons butter-flavored sprinkles
2 tablespoons grated Parmesan cheese
1 teaspoon dried basil, crushed
½ teaspoon dried parsley flakes, crushed
⅛ to ¼ teaspoon garlic powder

Scout housewares departments for clear glass bottles. A 4-ounce size will hold this recipe.

1 In a small bowl combine butter-flavored sprinkles, Parmesan cheese, basil, parsley flakes, and garlic powder. Transfer mixture to a 4-ounce bottle. Cover and store mix in the refrigerator for up to 1 month. Makes enough to season 10 cups popped popcorn.

To present this gift you will need:
Bag of popcorn
Fabric napkin
Seasoning mix
Small clear glass jar with stopper
Raffia
2 ears of popcorn
Scissors
Decorative paper
Paper punch

TO PRESENT THIS GIFT... Wrap the bag of popcorn in the napkin. Place the seasoning mix in a small clear jar with a stopper or lid. Tie raffia around the bottle neck. Tie ears of popcorn to the bag with raffia.

For the tag, cut a rectangle from the paper. Fold in half. Punch a hole in one corner. Thread a piece of raffia through the hole.

also try this...

For a full night of fun, tuck video rental gift certificates into the raffia bow with the corn.

For a honey of a friend, fill a jar with this luscious sweet-and-spicy spread, then decorate the gift with glistening jewels that resemble drops of golden honey.

bejeweled jar

spiced honey butter

1 cup butter or margarine, softened
½ cup honey
1 teaspoon ground cinnamon

English muffins, whole wheat toast, corn-bread muffins—you name it! This luscious spread transforms just about any breakfast bread into a sweet, spicy treat.

1 In a mixing bowl beat butter or margarine, honey, and cinnamon with an electric mixer on medium speed until light and fluffy. Transfer to 1 or 2 storage containers. Cover and store in the refrigerator for up to 1 week. Serve at room temperature. Makes 1½ cups butter.

TO PRESENT THIS GIFT... Wash and dry jar. Use toothpick to apply small dabs of adhesive randomly to sides of jar. Press the jewels onto the adhesive. Glue a cluster of dried flowers to the jar lid. Let the adhesive dry.

For the tag, cut the green and yellow papers into small rectangular shapes using straight-edge scissors. Trim the yellow paper slightly smaller. Cut the bottom edge of the yellow paper using decorative-edge scissors. Glue yellow paper on the green, leaving more space at the bottom of the tag. Glue three evenly spaced jewels across the bottom. Let the glue dry. Punch a hole in the tag to insert the ribbon. Tie around the neck of the jar.

also try this...

Add jewels to the handle of a spreader as done for the jar and tag.

To present this gift you will need:
Small jar
Toothpick
Silicone glue
Gold jewels
Dried flowers
Decorative paper in green and yellow
Straight-edge and decorative scissors
Paper punch
Ribbon

Peanut Butter Brownie,
page 57

wishes

bright
birthday
wishes

take-out
temptations

Tuck these airy macaroons into a take-out box that shouts "Happy Birthday" with its streamer and confetti stickers.

TO MAKE THE RECIPE...

4 egg whites
4 cups sifted powdered sugar
2 cups chopped hickory nuts, black walnuts, or toasted pecans

hickory nut macaroons

It's amazing how just three ingredients stack up to a delightful, melt-in-your-mouth gourmet cookie. Feel free to vary the nuts used. Each option will give its own distinctive flavor to the treats.

1 In a large mixing bowl beat egg whites with an electric mixer on high speed until stiff, but not dry, peaks form. Gradually add powdered sugar, about ¼ cup at a time, beating at medium speed just until combined. Then beat 1 to 2 minutes more or until well combined. Fold in the nuts by hand.

2 Drop mixture by rounded teaspoons 2 inches apart onto parchment-lined or foil-lined cookie sheets (grease foil).

3 Bake in a 325° oven about 15 minutes or until edges are very light brown.* Transfer cookies to wire racks and let cool. Store in a tightly covered container at room temperature for up to 3 days or in the freezer for up to 3 months. Makes 36 cookies.

*Note: It is normal for these cookies to split around the edges as they bake.

TO PRESENT THIS GIFT... First decide on the arrangement of the stickers. Apply stickers to the sides of the container. Line box with tissue paper and fill with macaroons. Tie noisemaker to container's handle using a ribbon. To curl ribbon, carefully pull ribbon across a scissor blade.

also try this...

Add stickers to the outside edges of the tissue paper for a more decorative liner.

To present this gift you will need:
Stickers in desired shapes and colors
Plastic Chinese food container (available in paper supply stores)
Tissue paper
Noisemaker
Curling ribbon

colorful candy caddy

Drop sprightly lemon candies into an antique juicer—or any green-glass collectible—for a gift that's as sunny and bright as a spring morning.

lemon crunch candy

1 pound vanilla-flavored candy coating, cut up
¾ cup finely crushed hard lemon candies

Why wait until Christmas to enjoy goodies made with candy coating? Paired up with a sprinkling of lemon-yellow candy, the confection takes on a bright, fresh appeal that's perfect for a spring birthday.

1 Line a baking sheet with foil; set aside. In a heavy 2-quart saucepan heat candy coating over low heat, stirring constantly, until melted and smooth. Remove from heat. Stir in crushed candies, reserving some to sprinkle on top. Pour mixture onto the prepared baking sheet. Spread to about ⅜-inch thickness. Sprinkle with the reserved crushed candy pieces.

2 Chill candy about 30 minutes or until firm. (Or let candy stand at room temperature several hours or until firm.) Use foil to lift firm candy from the baking sheet; carefully break candy into pieces. Store tightly covered for up to 2 weeks. Makes 1 pound candy.

TO PRESENT THIS GIFT... Tie a ribbon bow around the handle of the juicer. Trim the ribbon ends. Arrange the candy pieces in the bowl portion of the juicer.

also try this...

At flea markets and antiques stores, look for other vessels that can be used as gift containers. Good examples include tumblers, sherbet glasses, sifters, and colanders.

To present this gift you will need:
⅛-inch-wide yellow ribbon
Antique juicer (find at antiques stores or flea markets)
Scissors

gift from the hearth

This loaf of home-baked bread symbolizes the warmth of friendship. The plaid napkin wrap, which can be used as a bread cloth, adds a homespun appeal.

FOR 1½-POUND LOAF
- ½ cup water
- ⅓ cup tomato juice
- ½ cup coarsely shredded carrots
- 2 tablespoons coarsely chopped sweet green pepper
- 2 tablespoons sliced green onion
- 1 tablespoon butter, margarine, or cooking oil
- 3 cups bread flour
- 1 teaspoon sugar
- ¾ teaspoon salt
- ¼ teaspoon dried basil, crushed
- 1 teaspoon active dry yeast or bread machine yeast*

FOR 2-POUND LOAF
- ⅔ cup water
- ½ cup tomato juice
- ⅔ cup coarsely shredded carrots
- 3 tablespoons coarsely chopped sweet green pepper
- 3 tablespoons sliced green onions
- 4 teaspoons butter, margarine, or cooking oil
- 4 cups bread flour
- 1½ teaspoons sugar
- 1 teaspoon salt
- ½ teaspoon dried basil, crushed
- 1 teaspoon active dry yeast or bread machine yeast*

garden bread

Be sure to tell the recipient that this loaf is perfect for toasted cheese sandwiches. In fact, if you'd like to add a little something extra to this gift, you could tuck in a wedge of imported cheddar or another cheese that toasts well.

1 Select the loaf size. Add the ingredients to a bread machine according to the manufacturer's directions. Select the basic white bread cycle. To store, wrap in foil or plastic wrap and store in a cool, dry place. Freeze any portion not consumed the first day. Makes a 1½- or 2-pound loaf.

*Note: Our Test Kitchen recommends 1 teaspoon yeast for either size loaf.

Lay the napkin flat and fold two opposite corners inward. Fold the long edges in again to shape a long narrow band of fabric. Lay the bread loaf in the center and bring the ends together. Secure with a napkin ring.

For the tag, cut a rectangle from art paper. Tear a smaller rectangle from brown paper. Glue brown paper on art paper. Let dry. Punch a hole in the corner. Thread ribbon through hole. Tie to napkin.

also try this...

Use a clean new fabric scarf to make the bread wrap.

To present this gift you will need:
- Clean purchased fabric napkin
- Coordinating napkin ring
- Scissors
- Art paper
- Brown craft paper
- Glue stick
- Paper punch
- ⅛-inch-wide ribbon

birthday wish
wands

Hooray!

Make birthday wishes come true **with magic wands made from candy-coated pretzel sticks. An appropriate container for such a multihued gift is, of course, a tin wrapped in rainbow-colored floss.**

TO MAKE THE RECIPE...

magic wands

2 cups chopped vanilla-flavored candy coating
2 tablespoons shortening
1 cup pretzel sticks
15 pretzel logs
Decorative colored sugars and small multicolored decorative candies
Paste food coloring

No mixing or baking required! Just stock up on artistic enthusiasm and lots of waxed paper to use while decorating.

1 In a heavy large saucepan heat candy coating and shortening over low heat, stirring constantly, until melted and smooth. Remove from heat; let stand 10 minutes. Gently stir in pretzel sticks. Remove coated pretzel sticks and arrange into star shapes on waxed paper. Sprinkle with colored sugar or decorative candies. Chill about 1 hour or until firm.

2 Meanwhile, to make wands, dip pretzel logs into the remaining melted candy coating. Shake off excess coating and place logs in a waxed paper-lined shallow baking pan. Sprinkle with decorative candies and add star tops, if desired, using some of the

remaining candy coating as "glue." Allow coating to set up.

3 If desired, tint any remaining coating with paste food coloring. Place in a heavy, self-sealing plastic bag; cut off a tiny corner of bag. Pipe melted colored candy coating onto dipped wands. Or dip coated end of dipped wand into a contrasting-color candy coating and sprinkle with colored sugar or decorative candies. Chill about 1 hour. To store, place wands in layers in an airtight container, separating layers with waxed paper. Store at room temperature for up to 1 week. Makes 15 wands and 15 stars.

TO PRESENT THIS GIFT...

Before painting, wash the container gently and dry it. Paint the outside of the container using black acrylic paint. Let dry. To hold the embroidery strands in place, use decoupage medium. Paint on the decoupage medium in rings as you work so it is wet when the floss is applied. Wrap floss over the wet decoupage medium, changing colors when desired. When the entire can is wrapped, paint another coat of decoupage medium over the outside of the container. Let dry. Line container with plastic wrap; fill with popcorn and wands.

For the tag, cut a triangle from white paper. Glue onto black paper and trim just beyond the white. Let dry. Cut a 12- and a 24-inch length of one floss color to wrap tassel. Using all colors of floss, wrap around 2 fingers approximately eight times. Slip the 12-inch length of floss through

the center of the floss bundle and tie tightly at the top. Use the remaining 24-inch length of floss to wrap the floss bundle, ¼ inch from where it is tied at the top. Knot and trim ends. Punch a hole in each corner of the paper triangle. Thread tassel ties through the bottom hole and one strand through each top hole. Knot ends together.

also try this...

A short crock from the flea market can also hold the birthday wands. Add color to the crock by wrapping with colorful rubber bands.

To present this gift you will need:
Metal tin, about 5 inches high by 4 inches wide
Black acrylic paint
Paintbrush
Decoupage medium
Cotton embroidery floss in desired colors
Plastic wrap
Popped popcorn
Scissors
Papers in white and black
Glue stick
Paper punch

gemlike delights

Sugar-sprinkled butter cookies sparkle like jewels under an inverted glass bowl, the perfect gift for a gem of a friend.

TO MAKE THE RECIPE...

¾ cup butter
½ cup granulated sugar
1 egg yolk
2 tablespoons milk
¼ teaspoon mint flavoring
2 cups all-purpose flour
Colored sugars (optional)

buttery mint cookies

For the stamped designs you see on page 48, look for cookie stamps in cookware catalogs or specialty cookware shops. The decorative bases of wine glasses also work well.

1 In a mixing bowl beat butter with an electric mixer on medium speed for 30 seconds. Add granulated sugar; beat until combined. Beat in egg yolk, milk, and mint flavoring. Beat in as much of the flour as you can with the mixer. Stir in any remaining flour with a wooden spoon. Cover and chill 2 hours or until easy to handle.

2 Shape dough into 1-inch balls. Place on an ungreased cookie sheet. Dip the bottom of a glass having a decorative base into colored sugar, if desired; use bottom of glass to flatten cookies.

3 Bake in a 350° oven for 8 to 10 minutes or until edges begin to brown. Transfer cookies to a wire rack to cool. Store in a tightly covered container at room temperature for up to 3 days or in the freezer for up to 3 months. Makes 42 cookies.

TO PRESENT THIS GIFT...

Stack the plates. Layer the cookies onto the plate, stacked so the inverted bowl fits on top. Place the bowl over the cookies. Wrap ribbon underneath the plate and tie at the top of the bowl. Tie a bow and trim the ribbon ends.

also try this...

Present the cookies on any plate that has a slight rim. Place a paper doily on the base before arranging the cookies.

To present this gift you will need:
Scalloped-edge decorative plates
Clear glass or plastic bowl that fits (upside down) on the plate
Sheer ribbon
Scissors

cornucopia
of candy

Transform a simple party hat into an elegant horn of plenty.
Nut-studded praline candy, gold ribbon, a doily, and a tassel do the trick.

¾ cup sugar
2 cups pecan pieces
3 tablespoons butter
1 teaspoon vanilla
⅛ teaspoon ground
cinnamon (optional)

praline crunch

While most anyone will delight in these caramely, crunchy candies, they make a particularly great gift for gourmet cooks. When chopped more finely, the pralines can be sprinkled into fruit salads, stirred into cooked sweet potatoes or squash, or used as a garnish for frosted cakes and brownies.

1 Butter a baking sheet; set aside. In a large skillet place sugar. Cook over medium-high heat, shaking pan occasionally, until sugar begins to melt. Reduce heat to low and cook until sugar is golden brown, stirring as necessary. Add pecans, butter, vanilla, and cinnamon, if desired. (Sugar may resolidify.) Stir to remelt sugar and coat nuts evenly.

2 Spread the mixture onto the prepared baking sheet. Cool completely. Break into small clusters. Store in a tightly covered container in a cool dry place for up to 3 weeks. Makes 10 to 12 servings.

In a well-ventilated work area, spray-paint the party hat silver. Let the paint dry. Wrap a gold doily around the hat, cutting to fit the cone shape. Glue in place. Let dry. Glue a plastic gem in the center of the doily. Add dots of glitter glue on and around the edge of the doily. Let dry. Slip the tassel ties through the hole at the tip of the hat. Tape the ends to the inside of the hat. Cut off the hat's elastic strap. Replace with a ribbon. You can staple the ribbon in place, or punch a hole on each side and thread the ribbon through the holes. Line the hat with parchment paper or waxed paper to keep food from coming into contact with painted surfaces; fill hat with Praline Crunch.

also try this...

For a child's party, use purchased party hats and fill with jelly beans or other favorite candies.

To present this gift you will need:
Silver spray paint
Paper party hat
Round gold doily
Scissors
Thick white crafts glue
½-inch round plastic gem
Silver glitter glue
Purchased tassel
Tape
Ribbon
Stapler or paper punch
Parchment paper or waxed paper

chocolate-lover's loaf

Wrap up this decadent cakelike bread with art paper and curling ribbon, and surprise the inveterate chocolate lover with yet another way to enjoy this cherished flavor.

chocolate buttermilk loaves

1²/₃ cups all-purpose flour
²/₃ cup unsweetened cocoa powder
½ teaspoon baking powder
½ teaspoon baking soda
½ teaspoon salt
½ cup butter, softened
1 cup sugar
2 eggs
1 cup buttermilk
⅓ cup chopped pecans or walnuts
¼ cup miniature semisweet chocolate pieces

Although it's technically a quick bread, this treat was developed with sweet tooths in mind. Note that the loaves will need to be taken out of the pans to cool, as directed in step three. After cooling thoroughly, you can present them in clean disposable pans if you wish.

1 Grease the bottom and ½ inch up the sides of four 5³/₄×3×2-inch foil loaf pans; place each in a shallow baking pan and set aside. In a medium mixing bowl combine flour, cocoa powder, baking powder, baking soda, and salt; set aside.

2 In a large mixing bowl beat the butter with an electric mixer on medium speed for 30 seconds. Add sugar and beat until fluffy. Beat in eggs until combined. Alternately add the flour mixture and buttermilk, beating just until combined after each addition. Stir in nuts. Spoon about ½ cup of the batter into each prepared pan. Sprinkle each pan with some of the chocolate pieces. Spoon on remaining batter.

3 Bake in a 350° oven for 30 to 35 minutes or until a wooden toothpick inserted near centers comes out clean. Cool in pans on wire racks for 10 minutes. Remove loaves from pans; cool completely on wire racks. Wrap tightly and store at room temperature for up to 3 days or in the freezer for up to 1 month. Makes 4 loaves.

Place loaves in clean pans. Pleat the art paper up around the sides of the pan. Cut three desired colors of curling ribbon into 18-inch lengths. Tie the paper at the top using curling ribbons and chenille stems, as desired. Use a scissor blade to curl each ribbon end.

also try this...

Use chenille stems to secure the paper by twisting them around the paper and then wrapping the ends of the stems around a pencil to curl them. Remove pencil.

To present this gift you will need:
Clean bread pans
Art paper
Scissors
Curling ribbon
Chenille stems

fishbowl of fun

Anglers in your life will get hooked on this delicious cracker mix—especially when you present it in a fishbowl with little goldfish swimming up the side.

cracker mix

- 1 cup bite-size fish-shape pretzel crackers or cheese-flavored crackers
- 1 cup oyster crackers
- 1 cup bite-size rich round crackers
- 1 cup bite-size shredded wheat biscuits
- 2 tablespoons cooking oil
- ½ teaspoon Worcestershire sauce
- ⅛ teaspoon garlic powder
  Dash bottled hot pepper sauce
- 2 tablespoons grated Parmesan cheese

Chances are, these nibbles will be gone before the party's over. If they're not, tell the recipient to cover the bowl tightly with plastic wrap to keep them fresh.

1 In a large bowl combine all crackers. In a small bowl combine oil, Worcestershire sauce, garlic powder, and bottled hot pepper sauce; pour over cracker mixture, tossing to coat. Sprinkle cracker mixture with Parmesan cheese; toss to coat. Spread mixture in a shallow baking pan.

2 Bake in a 300° oven for 10 to 15 minutes or until golden, stirring once. Cool completely. Store in an airtight container at room temperature for up to 2 weeks. Makes 4 cups cracker mix.

Cut three colored squares of decorative paper, each 8×8 inches (or larger or smaller, depending on the size of your fishbowl). Layer the papers with corners staggered. Place papers on top of the filled fishbowl. Tie a generous piece of black leather cord around the neck of the fishbowl to secure paper. Glue three fish crackers onto each tail of the black cord. Let glue dry.

also try this...

For single servings, use small jars or inexpensive glasses for the containers.

To present this gift you will need:
Decorative paper in 3 colors
Pinking shears
Glass or plastic fishbowl
Black leather cord
Extra fish crackers
Thick white crafts glue
Fish crackers

birthday
brownie surprise

A simple plastic food container makes a dandy dome and tray
for this peanut butter-glazed, candy-topped brownie.

TO MAKE THE RECIPE...

peanut butter brownie

¼ cup butter
2 ounces unsweetened
   chocolate, chopped
3 tablespoons creamy
   peanut butter
1 egg, beaten
¾ cup sugar
½ cup all-purpose flour
½ teaspoon vanilla
1 recipe Peanut Butter
   Glaze
⅓ cup chopped
   assorted candies,
   such as bite-size
   chocolate-covered
   peanut butter cups,
   candy-coated
   chocolate and peanut
   butter pieces,
   chocolate-coated
   caramel-topped
   nougat bars with
   peanuts, and/or small
   decorative candies

Know someone who's nuts about a particular kind of candy bar? Personalize this gift by sprinkling her favorite chopped bite-size bits on the top.

1 Grease a 6-inch springform pan. Set aside.

2 In a heavy small saucepan melt butter and chocolate over low heat, stirring frequently. Stir in peanut butter. Cool about 10 minutes. In a medium mixing bowl stir together the beaten egg, sugar, flour, and vanilla. Stir in the cooled chocolate mixture. Pour mixture into the prepared baking pan.

3 Bake in a 350° oven for 35 minutes. Cool for 10 minutes on a wire rack. Loosen sides of springform pan. Cool brownie completely.

4 Remove sides of springform pan and, using a thin metal spatula or knife, loosen bottom of brownie from bottom of pan. Carefully transfer brownie to a flat plate or a 7- or 8-inch cardboard round that's covered with foil.

5 Prepare Peanut Butter Glaze. Pour warm glaze over cooled brownie, spreading evenly and allowing it to drip down sides. Top with assorted candies. Store in a tightly covered container in the refrigerator for up to 3 days (or freeze unglazed brownie for up to 1 month). Makes 1 brownie.

Peanut Butter Glaze: In a heavy small saucepan melt 2 tablespoons creamy peanut butter and 1 tablespoon butter over low heat. Remove from heat and stir in ¾ cup sifted powdered sugar. Stir in 2 teaspoons very hot water. Stir in additional hot water, 1 teaspoon at a time, to make a glaze.

TO PRESENT THIS GIFT...

Turn the bowl portion of the plastic container upside down. Use paint pens to make scallops or other desired designs on the bottom and sides of the container as if decorating a birthday cake. Let dry. Use an ice pick to poke holes in a circle around the bottom (now the top) of the container. Put the candleholders into the holes. Put birthday candles into the holders.

also try this...

Press small rhinestones into the wet paint pen to add sparkle to the container design.

**To present
   this gift you
   will need:**
7- to 8-inch round
   plastic food
   container
Paint pens in desired
   colors
Ice pick
Birthday cake
   candleholders
Birthday candles

sunrise surprise

For a gift that really rises and shines, **wrap a container in decorative paper and fill it with homemade pancake mix.**

buttermilk pancake mix

8 cups all-purpose flour
2 cups buttermilk powder
½ cup sugar
2 tablespoons plus 2 teaspoons baking powder
4 teaspoons baking soda
2 teaspoons salt

If you like, present this gift with a bottle of your favorite syrup.

1 In a large mixing bowl combine flour, buttermilk powder, sugar, baking powder, baking soda, and salt. Stir until combined. Store in an airtight container in a cool, dry place for up to 6 weeks or in a freezer container in the freezer for up to 6 months. Makes about 10 cups.

Cut red decorative paper so it wraps around container with the edges overlapping slightly. Trim excess paper. Lay decorative paper on flat work surface. Spray adhesive on back side of the paper. Apply paper to container. To make wheat-stamped accent paper, tear a wide band from gold art paper to apply to the center of the container. Lay the paper, right side up, on a work surface. Load stamp with ink and press onto the paper as many times as desired, turning the stamp in various directions. Let ink dry. Turn the paper over and spray with adhesive. Apply paper to the center of container. Let dry. Trace around lid on a piece of stamped paper. Cut out circle. Spray the back side with adhesive and affix to container lid. Let dry.

For the tag, cut and fold a small rectangular tag from decorative paper scraps. Punch a hole in one corner. Tie the gift tag onto the container using a strand of raffia. Include preparation directions, below, with the gift.

also try this...
Delete the stamping process and use wrapping paper to cover the container.

To present this gift you will need:
Scissors
Red decorative paper
Cylinder-shape container that holds 10 cups
Spray adhesive
Gold art paper
Wheat stamp or desired design
Ink pad in desired color
Decorative paper scraps
Paper punch
Raffia

PREPARATION DIRECTIONS

buttermilk pancakes

2 eggs, slightly beaten
1⅔ cups water
⅓ cup margarine or butter, melted, or cooking oil
2½ cups Buttermilk Pancake Mix

1 Combine eggs, water, and margarine or butter or oil. Add Buttermilk Pancake Mix. Stir just until combined but still slightly lumpy. Heat a lightly greased griddle or heavy skillet over medium heat until a few drops of water dance across the surface. For each pancake, pour about ¼ cup batter onto the hot griddle. Spread batter into a circle about 4 inches in diameter.

2 Cook over medium heat until pancakes are golden brown, turning to cook second sides when pancake surfaces are bubbly and edges are slightly dry (about 2 to 3 minutes per side). Serve immediately or keep warm in a loosely covered ovenproof dish in a 300° oven. If desired, serve with your favorite syrup or topping. Makes 16 pancakes.

towering
tangerine trio

Sparkling gold jars of homemade marmalade **stack up to a striking gift when wrapped in ribbons and topped off with a tea ball.**

TO MAKE THE RECIPE...

10 to 12 tangerines
7 cups sugar
½ of a 6-ounce package liquid fruit pectin (1 pouch)

tangerine marmalade

Why do we invert the jars during part of the cooling time? Doing so helps prevent the peel from floating to the top.

1 Peel tangerines, reserving peel. Section fruit over a bowl to catch juice; discard membrane from sections. Dice fruit, removing seeds (you should have 3 cups pulp and ¾ cup juice). Scrape excess white from peel. Cut enough of the peel into very thin strips to make ¾ cup.

2 In an 8- to 10-quart Dutch oven or kettle combine diced pulp, juice, peel, and sugar. Bring to a full rolling boil. Quickly stir in pectin; return to a full boil. Boil for 1 minute, stirring constantly. Remove from heat. Quickly skim off foam with a metal spoon.

3 Immediately ladle into hot, sterilized half-pint or 4-ounce canning jars, leaving ½-inch headspace. Wipe jar rims and adjust lids. Process the filled jars in a boiling-water canner for 5 minutes (start timing when water begins to boil). Remove jars from canner; cool on racks for 2 hours. Turn jars upside down; cool 2 hours more. Turn jars right side up. Marmalade may require up to 2 weeks to set. Makes 7 half-pints or fourteen 4-ounce jars marmalade.

TO PRESENT THIS GIFT...
Cut 1 yard of ribbon. Stack the three marmalade jars. Secure with ribbon and tie into a bow on the top of the stacked jars. Add a tea infuser to the bow, letting it hang off the side.

also try this...
Instead of a tea infuser, tie a small decorative serving spoon to one of the ribbons.

To present this gift you will need:
Scissors
Multicolor ribbon
Tea infuser

clever clusters

They'll never guess that inside this mod-looking box,
wrapped with a geometric pattern of colorful rubber bands,
awaits an old-fashioned candy-shop-style treat.

hazelnut and cherry caramel clusters

4 ounces white chocolate or white chocolate baking squares, chopped

1 tablespoon shortening

1½ cups coarsely chopped hazelnuts (filberts) or almonds, toasted

⅓ cup dried tart cherries or dried cranberries

12 vanilla caramels (about 4 ounces)

2 teaspoons butter

To toast the nuts, spread in a single layer in a shallow baking dish; bake in a 350° oven for 5 to 10 minutes or until light golden brown, stirring once or twice. Watch carefully so they don't burn.

1 Line a baking sheet with foil. Butter foil; set aside.

2 In a heavy small saucepan melt white chocolate and shortening over low heat, stirring constantly, until smooth. Remove from heat. Stir in hazelnuts and cherries or cranberries. Let stand for 10 minutes to allow mixture to set up slightly. Drop by rounded tablespoon onto the prepared baking sheet.

3 In another heavy small saucepan combine caramels and butter. Cook and stir over low heat until melted and smooth. Remove from heat. Drizzle over the chocolate-nut pieces. Let stand until firm. Remove clusters from foil and store in a tightly covered container at room temperature up to 3 days. Makes 18 pieces.

Place the clusters in a cellophane-lined box bottom. Cover with the lid. Place the rubber bands around the box, arranging in both directions to make a grid or plaid pattern.

For the tag, cut a small square from colored cardboard. Punch a hole in the center of one side. Place rubber bands around the tag edges. Loop one rubber band through the punched hole.

also try this...

To make the box more colorful, wrap the box lid with colored wrapping paper or use a colored box.

To present this gift you will need:
Clean, white paper box
Cellophane
Large colored rubber bands in different widths
Scissors
Colored cardboard
Paper punch

barbecue-
lover's bundle

Nestled into an unbreakable bowl, which comes in handy when basting, these barbecue essentials are sure to delight the grilling enthusiast: a basting brush, a peachy-keen grilling sauce, and a sturdy dish towel to help with cleanup.

peach and pepper grilling sauce

TO MAKE THE RECIPE...

2 cups chopped sweet red peppers
1 cup chopped onion
1 teaspoon crushed red pepper
2 cloves garlic, minced
1 tablespoon olive oil
4 pounds fresh peaches or three 16-ounce packages frozen unsweetened peach slices, thawed
1½ cups packed light brown sugar
1 5½-ounce can peach or apricot nectar
¼ cup rice vinegar
1 tablespoon lemon juice
1 tablespoon soy sauce
2 teaspoons grated fresh ginger
¼ teaspoon salt

Ever wonder what the difference between rice vinegar and rice wine vinegar is? Rice vinegar is made from fermented rice, while rice wine vinegar is made from fermented rice wine. They can be used interchangeably in most recipes.

1 In a large skillet cook sweet pepper, onion, crushed red pepper, and garlic in hot oil just until tender. Remove from heat.

2 Wash fresh peaches, if using. Peel and pit peaches. Place half of the fresh or frozen peaches in a food processor bowl or blender container. Cover and process or blend until peaches are very finely chopped. Transfer chopped peaches to a 6-quart Dutch oven or kettle. Repeat with remaining peaches (you should have 7 cups finely chopped peaches). Process or blend the pepper mixture until finely chopped. Transfer to the Dutch oven with peaches. Add brown sugar, nectar, vinegar, lemon juice, soy sauce, ginger, and salt. Bring to boiling; reduce heat. Simmer, uncovered, for 15 to 20 minutes or until desired consistency, stirring occasionally. Remove from heat.

3 Immediately ladle hot sauce into hot, sterilized half-pint canning jars, leaving ¼-inch headspace. Wipe jar rims and adjust lids. Process the filled jars in a boiling-water canner for 15 minutes (start timing when water begins to boil). Remove jars from canner; cool on racks. Makes 7 half-pints sauce.

TO PRESENT THIS GIFT...

Measure the height and circumference of the jar lid. Cut a strip of brass this size. Use a paper punch to make a hole in the center of the strip every inch. Use an eyelet tool to secure an eyelet in each punched hole. Thread the ribbon through the eyelets. Tie the ends into a bow, securing brass ring around lid. Include preparation directions, below, with gift.

For the tag, cut a small tag from brass. Add a hole and eyelet at the top. Thread onto the ribbon before tying into a bow.

also try this...

Use colored leather cording or shoelaces instead of ribbon.

To present this gift you will need:
Ruler
Scissors to cut metal
Brass crafting metal
Paper punch
Silver eyelets and eyelet tool (available in the sewing notion department of crafts, discount, and fabric stores)
18-inch length of ¼-inch-wide ribbon

PREPARATION DIRECTIONS
Brush sauce over grilled or roasted meats or brush on beef, pork, or chicken during the last 5 minutes of grilling.

pretty.
pickles

Dress up jars of homemade pickles **with mesh** coverings that are cool, quick, and creative.

TO MAKE THE RECIPE...

- 4 pounds pickling cucumbers
- 8 cups sugar
- 4 cups cider vinegar
- 2 tablespoons mixed pickling spices
- 5 teaspoons pickling salt

sweet pickles

When you give this gift, you'll know you're giving a classic! The all-time favorite recipe came from a *Better Homes and Gardens®* reader in 1952. The pickling process takes a few days, but the results are worth it!

1 Wash cucumbers and place in a large bowl. Add boiling water to cover. Let stand, covered, at room temperature for 12 hours. Drain. Repeat procedure three more times.

2 Drain cucumbers and cut into ½-inch slices; place in an 8-quart nonmetal container. In a medium saucepan combine the sugar, vinegar, pickling spices, and salt; heat to boiling. Cook and stir to dissolve sugar. Pour over cucumber slices. Cover and let stand for 24 hours.

3 Transfer the cucumber mixture to an 8- to 10-quart Dutch oven or kettle. Heat to boiling. Remove from heat. Immediately fill hot, sterilized pint canning jars, leaving ½-inch headspace. Remove air bubbles, wipe jar rims, and adjust lids. Process the filled jars in a boiling-water canner for 10 minutes (start timing when water begins to boil). Remove jars from canner; cool on racks. Makes 8 pints pickles.

TO PRESENT THIS GIFT... Cut circles out of various papers to cover lids. Place paper circles on lids. Place a piece of netting over the lid, under the ring. Adjust ring on top of jar and trim off the extra netting to about ¾ inch all the way around.

For the tag, the metallic paper leaves were made by tracing a cucumber leaf onto paper and cutting them out. You can trace and cut a leaf as we did or cut out your own design. Punch a hole in the leaf and attach with colored wire around the neck of the jar. Curl ends of wire by wrapping tightly around a pencil, then remove the pencil.

also try this...

For the holidays, sew tiny jingle bells to the corners of the netting.

To present this gift you will need:
Scissors
Decorative paper
Gold netting
Metallic paper
Leaves in desired shapes
Pencil
Paper punch
Colored wire

birthday
celebration
sticks

A minigarden of candy-coated, **chocolate-dipped marshmallows blooms from a colorful flowerpot. Grow them for a sweet birthday gift or party favor.**

12 to 18 6- to 10-inch bamboo
    skewers
    Liquid food coloring
    (optional)
   36 large marshmallows
   ½ of a 24-ounce
    package chocolate- or
    vanilla-flavored candy
    coating (6 squares)
    Small multicolored
    decorative candies,
    finely chopped nuts,
    toasted coconut, ice
    cream nut topping,
    and/or almond toffee
    pieces (optional)
   4 ounces vanilla- or
    chocolate-flavored
    candy coating
    (2 squares) (optional)

double-dipped marshmallow sticks

Present the gift in the pot, as shown, but advise the recipient to wrap any uneaten sticks in airtight containers to store.

1 If desired, tint bamboo skewers with liquid food coloring. Thread 2 or 3 marshmallows on each bamboo skewer, leaving no space between them. Set aside.

2 In a medium saucepan heat the 12 ounces of candy coating over low heat until melted, stirring constantly. Remove from heat. Holding a skewer over the saucepan, spoon candy coating over marshmallows, spreading to coat evenly. If desired, sprinkle decorative candies, nuts, coconut, nut topping, and/or toffee pieces evenly over candy-coated marshmallow skewer. Place on waxed paper until set.

3 Or, if desired, for undecorated candy-coated marshmallows, in a small saucepan heat the 4 ounces of candy coating in a contrasting color over low heat until melted, stirring constantly. Remove from heat. Drizzle over assembled skewers.

4 When set, store in decorative airtight containers at room temperature for up to 1 week. Makes 12 to 18 skewers.

Gently press the foam ball into the flowerpot. Glue candy sprinkles on the outside of the flowerpot. Let the glue dry. Fill the top of the flowerpot with shredded paper. Push the ends of the marshmallow sticks into the foam ball to secure upright.

also try this...

Use small colored marshmallows instead of shredded paper to cover the foam ball after the sticks are inserted. (Make sure that the recipient knows that the colored marshmallows are for decorative purposes, and not to be eaten.)

**To present
   this gift you
   will need:**
Foam ball, such as
   Styrofoam
Colorful flowerpot
Thick white crafts glue
Candy sprinkles
Shredded paper

cheerful
cheese platter

A terrific-tasting cheese spread arrives all dressed for the party in a hand-painted cheese server topped with a pretty bow.

indian paneer cheese

12	cups whole milk
2	teaspoons salt
¼	teaspoon cumin seed, crushed
⅓	cup lemon juice

If you've ever eaten at an Indian restaurant and marveled at the fresh cheese sprinkled in salads and vegetables, chances are, that was paneer. Though out of the ordinary, it's surprisingly easy to make. It's also a great spread for flat bread.

1 In a 5-quart Dutch oven bring milk, salt, and cumin seed just to boiling; reduce heat. Simmer, uncovered, for 5 minutes. Remove from heat. Stir in lemon juice. Let stand 15 minutes.

2 Line a large strainer or colander with several layers of 100-percent-cotton cheesecloth. Strain mixture; discard liquid. Gently squeeze the cheesecloth to remove as much liquid from the curds as possible. Wrap cloth around curds. Place

wrapped curds in a large strainer or colander and put a weighted bowl on top to help press out any additional liquid. Let stand, covered, in the refrigerator for at least 15 hours.

3 Remove curds. Discard liquid. Form curds into a flat rectangle or press into a large bowl to shape. Refrigerate, covered with plastic wrap, until well chilled. Store in the refrigerator, tightly wrapped, for up to 3 weeks. Makes 1 pound cheese.

Wash and dry the cheese server. Avoid touching the areas to be painted. Place masking tape around the bottom of the cheese server lid, approximately ½ inch from the bottom edge. Paint a white stripe at the bottom of the lid, using the masking tape as a guide. Let the paint dry. Paint stripes of yellow over the white to create a checkerboard effect. Let the paint dry. Use orange paint to paint a thin line just below the tape. Paint the rim of the server base as desired using the same technique. Let the paint dry. Bake the painted glassware in the

oven if instructed by the paint manufacturer. Let cool. Tie a generous ribbon bow around the lid knob. Trim the ends, if necessary.

also try this...

Personalize the cheese server by painting a large initial on the side of the lid.

To present this gift you will need:
Cheese server with glass bottom or a glass plate
Masking tape
Small flat paintbrush
Glass paints in white, yellow, and light orange
Ribbon
Scissors

spirited bottles

When decorated from head to toe **with pearlized buttons,** tall glass bottles become sumptuous vessels for a luscious after-dinner liqueur.

almond cream liqueur

2 cups whipping cream
1 14-ounce can (1¼ cups) sweetened condensed milk or fat-free sweetened condensed skim milk
1 cup crème d'amande

When buying the whipping cream, be sure to check the date on the carton. You'll want to purchase cream that will still be fresh for up to 1 week after the gift is given.

1 In a large pitcher stir together the whipping cream, sweetened condensed milk, and liqueur. Pour into clean, decorative bottles. Cover and store in the refrigerator for up to 1 week. Makes about 4 cups liqueur.

Orange-Mocha Cream Liqueur: Prepare Almond Cream Liqueur as above except omit the crème d'amande and add ½ cup coffee liqueur, ¼ cup orange liqueur, and ¼ cup chocolate-flavored syrup. Combine all ingredients in a blender container or food processor bowl. Cover and blend or process just until smooth. Makes about 4 cups liqueur.

Use wire cutters to remove the shanks from any shank-type buttons. Decide if you want to make a pattern on the bottle or prefer a random design. Glue the buttons in place using silicone glue. Depending on the thickness of your glue, you may want to lay the bottle down on a towel until one side is dry. Then continue adding buttons, one side at a time. Let the glue dry. If the bottle has a cork stopper, glue buttons to the top. If the stopper has a ball, you may want to paint it. Let it dry. Fill bottle with liqueur. Include preparation directions, below, with gift.

also try this...

Use mismatched pieces of costume or flea market jewelry to embellish the bottles.

To present this gift you will need:
Wire cutters
Buttons
Frosted bottles
Silicone glue
Towel (optional)
Paintbrush (optional)
White pearl paint (optional)

PREPARATION DIRECTIONS
Stir or shake before serving over ice.

vienna cups

Coffee-flavored cookies presented in an elegant gold-beaded cup or mug remind the recipient of the richness of your friendship.

viennese coffee balls

If you're more of a crafter than a cook, this no-cook recipe is for you!

2	cups crushed shortbread cookies
1¼	cups sifted powdered sugar
1	cup finely chopped nuts
2	tablespoons unsweetened cocoa powder
1½	teaspoons instant coffee crystals or instant espresso powder
¾	teaspoon ground cinnamon
4 to 5	tablespoons brewed espresso or strong coffee, or water
½	cup sifted powdered sugar
	Sifted powdered sugar (optional)

1 In a large mixing bowl combine crushed cookies, the 1¼ cups powdered sugar, the nuts, cocoa powder, coffee crystals, and cinnamon. Add brewed espresso, coffee, or water, using just enough to moisten.

2 Form into 1¼-inch balls. Roll generously in the ½ cup powdered sugar. Place on a sheet of waxed paper and let stand until dry (about 1 hour). Store in a tightly covered container at room temperature for up to 3 days. Before serving, roll again in powdered sugar, if desired. Makes about 30 cookies.

Wrap gold beaded wire around the top portion of the mug, securing on the handle. To curl the ends of the beaded wire, wrap them around a pencil and remove pencil. Shape as desired. Cut a large square from cellophane. Place the cellophane in the mug and fill with coffee balls.

To present this gift you will need:
Gold beaded wire
Large clear glass mug
Round pencil
Clear cellophane

also try this...

Fill up a set of mugs and present on a coordinating serving tray.

tart in a jar

A jar of grandmotherly pie filling gets dressed up in lacy finery for a gift that's heartfelt and homespun.

TO MAKE THE RECIPE...

- 5 pounds fully ripe, firm nectarines or peaches
  Ascorbic acid color keeper
- 6 cups fresh blueberries
- 3½ cups sugar
- 1⅓ cups quick-cooking tapioca
- 1 teaspoon grated fresh ginger
- ½ teaspoon ground cinnamon
- ⅛ teaspoon ground nutmeg
- 2¼ cups water
- ¾ cup lemon juice

nectarine-blueberry pie filling

When nectarines and blueberries are at their peak, make up a batch of this filling. You'll have four birthday gifts on call all winter long.

1 Rinse nectarines; halve and remove pits. If using peaches, immerse in boiling water for 20 to 30 seconds or until skins begin to crack; remove and plunge into cold water. Slip off skins; halve and remove pits. Cut fruit into ½-inch slices. To prevent the fruit from darkening, treat it with ascorbic acid color keeper according to package directions. Measure 16 cups of nectarines or peaches. Rinse and drain blueberries. Set aside.

2 In an 8-quart Dutch oven or kettle heat about 6 cups water to boiling. Add half of the nectarines or peaches; return to boiling. Boil for 1 minute. Using a slotted spoon, transfer nectarines to a large bowl; cover. Repeat with remaining nectarines or peaches. Discard liquid from Dutch oven.

3 In the same kettle combine sugar, tapioca, ginger, cinnamon, and nutmeg. Stir in the 2¼ cups water. Let stand 5 minutes to allow tapioca to soften. Cook over medium-high heat, stirring constantly, until mixture thickens and begins to boil. Add lemon juice; boil 1 minute, stirring constantly. Immediately add nectarines or peaches and blueberries, stirring gently to coat. Cook and stir for 3 minutes or until heated through.

4 Immediately spoon hot fruit mixture into hot, sterilized quart canning jars, leaving 1½-inch headspace. Remove air bubbles, wipe jar rims, and adjust lids. Process the filled jars in a boiling-water canner for 30 minutes (start timing when water begins to boil). Remove jars from canner; cool on racks. Makes 4 quarts (enough for 4 pies or 40 tarts or turnovers).

TO PRESENT THIS GIFT... First measure the circumference and height of the jar. Use straight scissors to cut a piece of paper 1 inch wider and taller than the measured size. With the long edges together, fold the paper in half. Using pinking shears, make cuts through the fold every ¼ inch, leaving ¼ inch uncut at the ends. Unfold paper. Wrap paper piece around the jar, taping the ends together at top and bottom. Tie a ribbon bow around the top of the jar. Include preparation directions with gift.

also try this...

Make different designs in the cut-paper wrap by using a variety of decorative-edge scissors to cut the slits.

PREPARATION DIRECTIONS

Nectarine-Blueberry Pie: Prepare pastry for two-crust pie. Spoon 1 quart Nectarine-Blueberry Pie Filling into a pastry-lined 9 inch pie plate. Cut slits in top crust; adjust top crust. Seal and flute edge. Cover edge of pie with foil. Bake in a 375° oven for 25 minutes; remove foil. Bake 25 to 30 minutes more or until pastry is golden and filling is bubbly. Makes one 9-inch pie.

Nectarine-Blueberry Tarts or Turnovers: Prepare pastry for three single-crust pies. Divide dough into 10 equal pieces and form into balls. Roll each ball of dough into a 6-inch circle and place on an ungreased baking sheet. Use 1 quart Nectarine-Blueberry Pie Filling. For tarts, place about ⅓ cup filling in the center of each circle, spreading filling to about 1½ inches from edges. Bring pastry up and over filling, pleating as necessary, forming a border. For turnovers, spoon filling onto half of the pastry circle to about ¾ inch from edge. Fold other half of pastry up and over filling. Brush edges with a little milk and seal edges, crimping as desired. Using a sharp knife, make several small slits in the top of each turnover. If desired, brush tops with a mixture of 1 beaten egg white combined with 1 tablespoon water. Bake tarts or turnovers in a 375° oven about 30 minutes or until light brown. Makes 10 tarts or turnovers.

To present this gift you will need:
Tape measure
Straight-edge scissors
Decorative art paper
Pinking shears
Tape
Ribbon

fruits and
flowers

Spread some old-fashioned birthday cheer. **Present this colorful fruit-studded spread inside a sugar bowl made beautiful with a hand-painted flower motif.**

almond-raisin butter

½ cup golden raisins
1½ teaspoons finely shredded orange peel (set aside)
2 tablespoons orange juice
2 tablespoons sliced almonds, toasted
½ cup butter or margarine, softened

Tailor the fruit to match the colors you paint on the sugar bowl. Dried cranberries, dried blueberries, and dried tart red cherries all make excellent substitutes for the raisins. The spread tastes great on toast or pancakes.

1 In a blender container or food processor bowl combine raisins and orange juice. Cover and blend or process with several on-off turns (do not grind). Add almonds; cover and blend or process with several on-off turns until chopped. Set aside.

2 In a medium mixing bowl beat butter with an electric mixer on medium speed until light and fluffy. Add raisin mixture and orange peel; stir until combined. Cover and store in the refrigerator for up to 1 week. Serve at room temperature. Makes 1 cup.

Wash and dry the bowl and lid. Avoid touching the areas to be painted. Use paints and a paintbrush to enhance the bowl's established design. Use as many or as few colors as you desire. To make tiny dots, dip the handle end of a paintbrush into paints and dot onto the bowl. Let the paint dry. Bake the painted glassware in the oven if instructed by the paint manufacturer. Let cool.

also try this...

To add a flower motif to a plain bowl, dip the handle end of a paintbrush in paint and dot onto the bowl in a tiny circle to make a flower shape.

To present this gift you will need:
Sugar bowl with raised or recessed design
Glass paints in desired colors
Fine-line paintbrush

Flower Cookie Pops,
page 93

cherished
gifts for
all seasons

truffles from the heart

Champagne-infused truffles invite romance when cradled
inside a big-hearted cookie cutter atop a dainty doily base.

champagne truffles

6 ounces semisweet chocolate, coarsely chopped
¼ cup butter, cut into small pieces
3 tablespoons whipping cream
1 egg yolk, beaten
3 tablespoons champagne or whipping cream
Unsweetened cocoa powder, sifted powdered sugar, nonpareils, and melted white chocolate

For the most impressive results, choose the best imported chocolate for these special-occasion truffles. Prefer not to pop the cork just yet? Substitute any flavored liqueur, or more whipping cream, for the champagne.

1 In a heavy medium saucepan combine semisweet chocolate, butter, and 3 tablespoons whipping cream. Cook and stir constantly over low heat until chocolate is melted. Gradually stir about half of the hot mixture into the egg yolk; return entire mixture to the saucepan. Cook and stir over medium heat for 2 minutes. Remove from heat.

2 Stir in champagne or 3 tablespoons whipping cream. Transfer truffle mixture to a small bowl; chill about 1 hour or until completely cool and smooth, stirring occasionally.

3 Using an electric mixer on medium speed, beat cooled truffle mixture about 1 minute or until color lightens and mixture is slightly fluffy. Chill about

30 minutes more or until mixture holds its shape. Scrape a small ice cream scoop, melon baller, or spoon across the surface of the cold truffle mixture, forming 1-inch balls. Place balls on a baking sheet lined with waxed paper. Refrigerate until firm.

4 Roll balls in cocoa powder, powdered sugar, or nonpareils, or drizzle with melted white chocolate, as desired.

5 Refrigerate truffles, tightly covered, up to 2 weeks. Makes about 25 candies.

Carefully apply small dabs of glue to the back side of the doily. Press the doily onto the red paper, leaving at least ½ inch around edges. Let glue dry. Using the doily shape as a guide, trim the red paper ¼ inch beyond the doily using decorative-edge scissors. Turn the paper with the doily side up. Place the cookie cutter in the center of the doily. Tape the cookie cutter to the doily on the inside of the cutter. Line bottom of holder with waxed paper. Arrange truffles inside the cookie cutter.

also try this...

Add a Valentine's message on the edge of the cookie cutter. Use a gold or silver marking pen to write your sentiments.

To present this gift you will need:
Glue stick
Heart-shape paper doily, slightly larger than the cookie cutter
Bright red art paper
Decorative-edge scissors
Large, red, heart-shape cookie cutter
Tape
Waxed paper

lollipops
with
love

Cupid himself would be smitten **with this bouquet of lollipops that blossom out of a malt-shop glass. A puff of sparkling red garland adds a playful note.**

8 ounces assorted red, pink, and/or clear hard candies

35 to 60 (2 to 3 ounces) assorted small decorative candies, such as red cinnamon candies, small nonpareils, colored candy hearts, spice drops, and gumdrops
Lollipop sticks

"be mine" lollipops

No candy thermometer needed! Just crush some hard candies, bake, decorate, and cool for a sweetheart of a gift!

1 Place unwrapped hard candies in a heavy plastic bag, then place bag on top of a folded towel and crush candies into small chunks with a meat mallet or a small hammer.

2 Make only 2 or 3 lollipops at one time. Line a baking sheet with foil; lightly grease the foil. Use approximately 1½ to 2 tablespoons of the crushed candy per lollipop and place on foil. Candy layer should be ¼ to ½ inch thick. Add small decorative candies to crushed candies.

3 Bake in a 350° oven for 6 to 8 minutes or until candies are completely melted. Cool 30 seconds. Quickly attach a stick to the base of each lollipop, twisting the stick to cover lollipop end with melted candy. If desired, carefully press more small candies into hot lollipops. Cool. Peel foil from lollipops. Store, covered, in a cool, dry place for up to 1 week. Makes 8 lollipops.

Note: These lollipops are not intended for children under age 3.

Push small pieces of tissue paper into the glass until half filled. Arrange lollipops in glass. Wind garland around lollipop stems to hold in place.

also try this...
Flea market vases and tumblers work nicely as lollipop holders.

To present this gift you will need:
Red tissue paper
Tall ice cream glass
Red sparkling garland

floral fancy

Flowers or sweets? **Give both pleasures wrapped up in one with this buttery shortbread topped with edible blooms.**

TO MAKE THE RECIPE...

1¼ cups all-purpose flour
3 tablespoons granulated sugar
½ cup butter
1 tablespoon dried egg whites
2 tablespoons water
8 to 16 small edible pansies or other edible flowers
Fine sanding sugar

pansy shortbread

Containers of organically grown edible flowers are available year-round in most supermarkets. Before using the flowers, rinse and gently pat them dry. If edible pansies are not available, edible violas also work well.

1 In a medium mixing bowl combine flour and granulated sugar. Using a pastry cutter, cut in butter until mixture resembles fine crumbs and starts to cling. Form the mixture into a ball and knead until smooth.

2 Pat or roll the dough into a 7- to 8-inch circle on an ungreased cookie sheet. Using your fingers, press to make a scalloped edge. Cut circle into 8 to 16 wedges; do not separate.

3 Bake in a 325° oven for 30 to 35 minutes or until bottom just starts to brown and center is set. Cut circle into wedges again while warm. Cool on cookie sheet on a wire rack.

4 Combine dried egg whites and water. Brush tops of wedges with egg white mixture. Place pansies on top; brush with more egg mixture. Sprinkle with fine sanding sugar. Bake for 5 minutes more. Transfer to wire racks and cool. Store in a tightly covered container at room temperature for up to 3 days or in the freezer for up to 1 month. Makes 8 to 16 wedges.

TO PRESENT THIS GIFT... Choose a clear glass plate, large enough to hold shortbread wedges. Arrange the shortbread on the plate. Cut a 3-inch-wide strip of tulle ribbon, long enough to wrap around the plate and the shortbread. Tie the ribbon into a bow at the top. Trim the ribbon ends.

also try this...

After the shortbread is arranged on the plate, tuck more fresh edible flowers around the shortbread wedges.

To present this gift you will need:
Clear glass rectangular plate
Scissors
Lavender tulle ribbon

spring-colored
cookie bags

Whimsical is the word **for these colorful cookies tucked into a pretty bag with playfully oversize handles.**

TO MAKE THE RECIPE...

4½ cups all-purpose flour
1 teaspoon baking soda
1 teaspoon cream of tartar
1 teaspoon salt
1 cup butter
1 cup sifted powdered sugar
1 cup granulated sugar
1 cup cooking oil
2 eggs
2 teaspoons almond extract
Colored sugar (optional)
White baking pieces, melted (optional)
Paste food coloring (optional)
Edible confetti candies (optional)

polka-dot drops

Why save all the rich butter cookies for Christmas? Dressed in the right colors, these classics befit any season!

1 In a medium mixing bowl stir together the flour, baking soda, cream of tartar, and salt; set aside.

2 In a large mixing bowl beat butter with an electric mixer on medium-low speed until smooth. Add powdered sugar and granulated sugar; beat on medium-high speed until fluffy. Add oil, eggs, and almond extract; beat just until combined. Gradually add dry ingredients, beating on medium speed just until combined. Cover and chill about 30 minutes.

3 Shape dough into 1¼-inch balls. (The dough will be soft.) Arrange balls 2 inches apart on ungreased cookie sheets. With the palm of your hand or the bottom of a glass or a cookie stamp dipped in granulated sugar, gently flatten the balls to about ¼-inch thickness. If desired, sprinkle with colored sugar.

4 Bake in a 350° oven for 10 to 12 minutes or until edges are light brown. Transfer cookies to a wire rack to cool. If desired, tint melted baking pieces with food coloring; dip one edge of the plain cookies in the melted mixture and sprinkle with candies before coating sets. Store cookies in a tightly covered container at room temperature for up to 3 days or in the freezer for up to 3 months. Makes 55 to 60 cookies.

TO PRESENT THIS GIFT... Cut the original handle and cardboard top off the gift bag. Decorate the remaining bag with paint markers as desired. Fold the crafting foam in half and cut out a decorative handle. Punch two holes on either side of the top of the bag; punch corresponding pairs of holes into the foam handles. Thread a brad fastener through the prepunched foam handle and then into the prepunched bag. Repeat the process for the other side of the bag. Line bag with tissue paper, waxed paper, or parchment paper.

also try this...

If you don't have crafting foam, sandwich lightweight cardboard between felt for the handles.

To present this gift you will need:
Scissors
Paper or vellum gift bag
Paint markers
Crafting foam
Paper punch
4 brad fasteners
Tissue paper, waxed paper, or parchment paper

easter
pizza
package

Look what the Easter Bunny brought: A candy-topped cookie pizza and a beautiful pie server wrapped in the colors of spring.

1 20-ounce roll refrigerated sugar cookie dough, cut into ¼-inch slices
1 16-ounce can vanilla frosting
   Yellow paste food coloring
¼ cup flaked coconut
   Green food coloring
1½ cups jelly beans and/or egg-shaped candies

easter cookie pizza

This extra-easy and super-colorful recipe is a great choice if you want to get kids involved.

1 Press cookie dough slices into a greased 13-inch pizza pan. Bake in a 350° oven for 15 to 20 minutes or until golden. Cool completely on a wire rack.

2 Tint frosting with yellow food coloring. Spread over cooled cookie. Tint coconut with green food coloring. Sprinkle tinted coconut and candies over frosting before it sets. Store in a tightly covered container in the refrigerator for up to 3 days. Makes 12 servings.

Working in 1-inch sections at a time, place a small amount of glue on the pie server handle. Wrap with a chenille stem. Add more glue and a chenille stem of another color. Continue working in this manner until the entire handle of the pie server is covered with chenille stems. Let the glue dry. Tuck server between pizza and pan; wrap pizza with cellophane and tie with ribbon.

also try this...
Wrap the handle of the pie server with variegated yarn in Easter colors.

To present this gift you will need:
Thick white crafts glue
Pie server with a straight handle
Chenille stems in lime green, yellow, purple, pink, and orange
Cellophane
Ribbon

fresh-baked
blooms

A floral-stenciled flower box hints at what's inside. But there's a surprise—these blossoms are fresh-baked rather than fresh-picked!

TO MAKE THE RECIPE...

flower cookie pops

Ever hear the saying "pretty enough to eat"? Well, you will when your friends see these gorgeous garden-inspired goodies.

$2/3$ cup butter, softened
$1/2$ of an 8-ounce can almond paste, crumbled ($1/2$ cup)
$1/3$ cup sugar
2 teaspoons finely shredded orange peel or lemon peel
1 teaspoon baking powder
$1/2$ teaspoon salt
$1/4$ teaspoon almond extract
1 egg
$2 1/2$ cups all-purpose flour
Paste and liquid food coloring (optional)
Short wooden dowels
1 egg white, beaten
Sugar

1 In a large mixing bowl beat butter and almond paste with an electric mixer on medium to high speed about 1 minute or until combined. Add the $1/3$ cup sugar, the orange peel, baking powder, salt, and almond extract. Beat until combined, scraping sides of bowl occasionally. Beat in egg. Beat in as much of the flour as you can with the mixer. Stir in any remaining flour with a wooden spoon.

2 Divide dough into several portions. Work desired paste food coloring into each portion, if desired. Cover and chill for 1 hour or until easy to handle.

3 Grease cookie sheets; set aside. On a lightly floured surface roll half of the dough at a time to $3/8$-inch thickness. Cut into desired shapes using $2 1/2$- to $3 1/2$-inch cutters. (Or, if desired, shape flower cookies and leaves from dough.) Place cookies 1 inch apart on the prepared cookie sheets, staggering rows of cookies so that wooden dowels can be inserted into flower shapes. (If desired, stain dowels with green liquid food coloring.) Insert a wooden dowel $1/2$ inch into the bottom edge of each cookie. Brush cookies with egg white and sprinkle lightly with sugar.

4 Bake in a 375° oven for 8 to 10 minutes or until edges are firm and bottoms are very light brown. Cool on cookie sheet for 1 minute. Carefully transfer cookies to a wire rack and cool completely. Store in a tightly covered container at room temperature for up to 3 days or in the freezer for up to 3 months. Makes about 24 cookies.

TO PRESENT THIS GIFT...

Trace cookie cutter shapes onto the sponges. Cut out shapes. Soak sponges in water to expand. Squeeze out excess water. Place paints on paper plate. Dip sponges in desired paint colors. Sponge-paint the flowers on the flower box as desired. While the paint is wet, sprinkle with glitter. Tap off excess glitter. Paint stems and leaves. Let the paint dry. Line box and cover cookies with tissue paper. Place lid on box and tie with a ribbon bow. Trim the ribbon ends, if needed.

also try this...

Use seasonal cookie cutters to create holiday motifs such as bells, leaves, or snowflakes to embellish the box lid.

To present this gift you will need:
Pencil
Flower- and heart-shape cookie cutters
Flat crafts sponges
Scissors
Acrylic paints in pink, yellow, purple, green, or other desired colors
Paper plate
Flower box (available from floral shops)
White glitter
Paintbrush
Tissue paper
Ribbon

old-fashioned finery

A decoupage vintage candy jar **with nostalgic butterflies is the perfect parcel for a Victorian-style lemon curd.**

luscious lemon curd

1 cup sugar
1½ teaspoons cornstarch
4 teaspoons finely
shredded lemon peel
(set aside)
⅓ cup lemon juice
¼ cup butter, cut up
3 beaten eggs

Tart, tangy, and translucent, old-fashioned lemon curd is making a comeback. Make an extra batch for yourself to spread over scones, nestle between butter-cake layers, or spoon over gingerbread.

1 In a medium saucepan (do not use an aluminum pan) combine sugar, cornstarch, and lemon juice. Add butter. Cook and stir over medium heat until thickened and bubbly. Cook and stir for 2 minutes more.

2 Stir about half of the mixture into beaten eggs. Return all to saucepan. Reduce heat; cook and stir for 1 to 2 minutes more or until mixture

begins to thicken. Do not boil. Strain to remove any egg particles. Gently stir lemon peel into hot mixture and pour into small jars. Cool. Cover and store in the refrigerator for up to 1 month. Makes 1¾ cups spread.

TO PRESENT THIS GIFT... Wash and dry the candy jar and lid. Paint the underside of the lid with decoupage medium. While the lid is wet, tuck the napkin up into the lid, carefully pressing into place against decoupage medium. Trim away the excess napkin and fold the napkin up to make a smooth edge. Cut a few small motifs from the napkin and decoupage on the outside of the jar. Let the decoupage medium dry. Tie a ribbon around the jar lid knob. Be sure to cover the curd with plastic wrap to prevent it from coming into contact with the napkin and decoupage medium. Include preparation instructions, below, with gift.

For the tag, cut the watercolor paper to the desired size of the tag. Fold in half. Punch a hole near the fold. Decoupage a motif from the napkin in the center of the tag. Let dry. Add two marking-pen rules at the bottom of the tag, inside and out. Thread cord through holes and tie around jar top.

also try this...

Use small motifs from wrapping paper to embellish the jar and tag.

To present this gift you will need:
Candy jar with lid
Paintbrush
Decoupage medium
Paper napkin with dainty design
Scissors
Ribbon
Plastic wrap
Watercolor paper
Paper punch
Fine-line marking pen
Satin cord

PREPARATION DIRECTIONS

Serving Suggestion: Spoon Luscious Lemon Curd into baked miniature phyllo shells and garnish with wedges of kiwi fruit and fresh blueberries.

early-summer
treasure

Preserve the sweetness of summer's fresh cherry season in a delightful jam you can give all year long.

sweet cherry jam

3 pounds fully ripe dark sweet cherries
1 1¾-ounce package regular powdered fruit pectin
1 teaspoon finely shredded lemon peel
¼ cup lemon juice
5 cups sugar

A cherry pitter, available from a cookware shop or catalog, removes pits from cherries easily. If you don't have a pitter, halve the cherries, then pry the pits out with the tip of a knife.

1 Sort, wash, stem, pit, and chop cherries. Measure 4 cups chopped cherries.

2 In a 6- or 8-quart Dutch oven or kettle combine cherries, pectin, lemon peel, and lemon juice. Bring to boiling over high heat, stirring constantly. Stir in sugar. Bring to a full rolling boil. Boil hard for 1 minute, stirring constantly. Remove from heat. Quickly skim off foam with a metal spoon.

3 Immediately ladle hot jam into hot, sterilized half-pint canning jars, leaving ¼-inch headspace. Wipe jar rims and adjust lids. Process the filled jars in a boiling-water canner for 5 minutes (start timing when water begins to boil). Remove jars from canner; cool on racks. Makes 6 half-pints jam.

On the wrong side of the wrapping paper, trace around the jar lid. Cut out a circle 1½ inches beyond the pencil mark. Cut scallops along edge of paper. Clip into edges evenly every ¾ inch, clipping only to the jar lid line. Place paper circle on lid, under ring, and adjust ring on top of jar.

For the tag, cut a rectangle from coordinating paper. Punch stars in where desired. Punch a hole in one corner for ribbon tie. String ribbon through tag and tie around lid. If desired, include a glass jam serving dish and spoon with the gift.

also try this...

Use bright-colored patterned origami papers for one-of-a-kind lid toppers.

To present this gift you will need:
Wrapping paper
Pencil
Scissors
Paper
Star-shape paper punch
Ribbon
Glass jam serving dish (optional)
Gold or silver serving spoon (optional)

key lime combo

Fudge becomes a jewel of a gift that's suitable for any festive occasion thanks to the spark of Key lime flavor and the sparkle of a sequin-trimmed doily.

TO MAKE THE RECIPE...

key lime fudge

- 3 cups white baking pieces
- 1 14-ounce can (1¼ cups) sweetened condensed milk
- 2 teaspoons finely shredded lime peel
- 2 tablespoons bottled Key lime juice or regular lime juice
- 1 cup chopped macadamia nuts, toasted if desired

If you wish, you can substitute fresh Key lime juice or regular lime juice for the bottled juice. Fresh Key limes can be found in Hispanic markets.

1 Line an 8×8×2- or 9×9×2 inch baking pan with foil, extending foil over edges of pan. Butter foil; set aside.

2 In a heavy large saucepan stir baking pieces and sweetened condensed milk over low heat just until pieces are melted and mixture is smooth. Remove from heat. Stir in lime peel and lime juice. Stir in macadamia nuts.

3 Spread mixture evenly into the prepared pan. If desired, sprinkle a few additional coarsely chopped macadamia nuts over the top. Cover and chill for 2 hours or until firm.

4 Lift fudge from pan using edges of foil. Peel off foil. Use a knife to cut into pieces. Store in an airtight container at room temperature for up to 1 week or in the freezer for up to 2 months. Makes 2½ pounds fudge.

TO PRESENT THIS GIFT...
Glue the sequin string around the edge of the doily. Continue gluing the sequins around the doily until the circle is complete. Trim the excess. Let the glue dry. Place the doily on a cut-glass plate; stack fudge on top of doily.

also try this...
Replace the doily with a piece of art paper that has been cut into a circle using decorative-edge scissors.

To present this gift you will need:
Thick white crafts glue
Sequins on a string
Paper doily
Scissors
Cut-glass plate

pit master's
provisions

Master barbecuers will get a kick out of **this sprinkle-top jar of homemade barbecue rub. It's twice as nice planted among flavored hardwood chips in a decorated terra-cotta pot.**

spicy barbecue rub

2 tablespoons brown sugar
1 tablespoon granulated sugar
1 tablespoon ground allspice
1 tablespoon ground ginger
1 teaspoon salt
1 teaspoon ground cumin
1 teaspoon ground red pepper
1 teaspoon ground black pepper

Spices lose their flavor after a year. To ensure that your gift stays fresh for the 6 months indicated, use spices that have been purchased in the last 6 months.

1 In a small mixing bowl stir together the brown sugar, granulated sugar, allspice, ginger, salt, cumin, red pepper, and black pepper. Transfer to a small airtight container or bag. Store at room temperature for up to 6 months. Makes about ⅓ cup seasoning.

TO PRESENT THIS GIFT... Paint vertical green stripes below the rim of the flowerpot. Let dry. Paint the letters "BBQ" around the rim in red. Let the paint dry. Cut and tie a ribbon around the top of the flowerpot. Tie the ends into a bow. Cut a 6-inch square from two colors of art paper using pinking shears. Take the lid off the barbecue rub. Place plastic wrap over the jar rim, then place the papers on top of the jar and carefully screw the lid back on (the plastic wrap will help keep the contents fresh). Fill the flowerpot with hardwood chips for grilling and place the jar of rub inside. Include preparation directions, below, with gift.

also try this...
Fill the flowerpot with shredded paper or Mylar before adding the jar.

To present this gift you will need:
Paintbrush
Acrylic paints in red and green
Terra-cotta flowerpot
Scissors
Narrow ribbon
Colored art papers
Pinking shears
Plastic wrap
Hardwood chips for grilling

PREPARATION DIRECTIONS

To use, sprinkle mixture evenly over meat, poultry, or fish. Rub in with your fingers. Grill as desired. If you like, serve with bottled chutney, barbecue sauce, sweet and sour sauce, or plum sauce.

pickle parcel

Use a potato to hand-stamp the leaf motif on this beautiful bag. Inside, tuck a bounty of dilled delights worthy of a state-fair prize.

TO MAKE THE RECIPE...

pickled dilled green beans

For the best flavor, let these beans stand in a cool, dark place for 2 weeks before using.

- 3 pounds green beans
- 5 desired fresh hot peppers (such as red serrano peppers) (optional) (see note, page 25)
- 3 cups water
- 3 cups white wine vinegar
- 1 tablespoon pickling salt
- 1 tablespoon sugar
- 3 tablespoons snipped fresh dillweed or 3 teaspoons dried dillweed, crushed
- ½ teaspoon crushed red pepper
- 6 cloves garlic, minced
- 5 small heads fresh dill (optional)

1 Wash beans; drain. Trim ends, if desired. Place enough water to cover beans in an 8-quart Dutch oven or kettle. Heat to boiling. Add beans and fresh peppers, if desired, to the boiling water; return to boiling. Boil, uncovered, for 5 minutes. Drain.

2 Immediately pack beans lengthwise into hot, sterilized pint canning jars, cutting beans to fit if necessary and leaving ½-inch headspace. Place one hot pepper (if using) into each jar so that it shows through the glass. Set aside.

3 In a large saucepan combine the 3 cups water, the vinegar, pickling salt, sugar, dillweed, crushed red pepper, and garlic. Bring to boiling. Pour over beans in jars, leaving ½-inch headspace. If desired, add fresh dill to jars. Remove air bubbles, wipe jar rims, and adjust lids. Process the filled jars in a boiling-water canner for 5 minutes (start timing when water begins to boil). Remove jars from canner; cool on racks. Makes 5 pints pickled beans.

TO PRESENT THIS GIFT...

Cut a potato in half. Cut away some of the potato at flat end to carve a leaf shape. Cut leaf vein lines into the leaf shape. Dry off potato with paper towel. Spread green and ivory paint evenly onto plate. Dip potato stamp into paint and stamp a few times onto a scrap paper first, then stamp pattern onto bag. Let dry. To make a topper for each jar, crease folds into paper. Trace around jar lid and cut out. Place paper on lid under lid ring and adjust ring on top of jar. Tie raffia at the top and add a sprig of your favorite herb.

also try this...

Write the recipe name on a purchased gift tag as a reminder of the jar's contents.

To present this gift you will need:
Knife
Medium-size potato
Paper towel
Acrylic paints in green and ivory
Disposable foam plate
Scrap paper
Paper bag in desired color
Paper for jar tops
Pencil
Raffia
Herb sprig

sumptuous
syrup

Give the gift of elegance. Luscious blueberry syrup presented in a striking ribboned and jeweled cruet will make a splendid start to any day.

TO MAKE THE RECIPE...

2 cups fresh or frozen
  blueberries
½ cup water
⅓ cup sugar
2 teaspoons lime juice
  or lemon juice

blueberry syrup

This not-too-sweet syrup is loaded with whole berries. For two times the pleasure, present it with the homemade pancake mix gift on page 59.

1 In a medium saucepan combine 1 cup of the blueberries, the water, sugar, and lime or lemon juice. Cook and stir over medium heat for 2 to 3 minutes or until sugar dissolves. Bring to boiling; reduce heat. Simmer, uncovered, for 15 to 20 minutes or until slightly thickened, stirring occasionally.

2 Stir in the remaining 1 cup blueberries and cook, stirring occasionally, 2 to 3 minutes more or until blueberries become soft. Cover and refrigerate syrup for up to 1 week. Makes 1 cup syrup.

TO PRESENT THIS GIFT...

Glue a gem or flat button on the top of stopper. Let the glue dry. Fill the cruet with syrup. Wipe off any excess from the outside of the bottle. Top bottle with stopper. String beads onto narrow ribbon, knotting at each end to secure the beads. Tie a generous bow from wide ribbon around the neck of the bottle. Tie the strung beads around the neck of the bottle. Include preparation instructions, below, with gift.

also try this...

String the beads on medium-weight craft wire and curl the ends into spirals.

PREPARATION DIRECTIONS

To serve, heat in a saucepan just until warm. Spoon over waffles, pancakes, or ice cream.

To present this gift you will need:

Small cruet with glass
  stopper
Silicone glue
Gem or flat decorative
  button
Colorful coordinating
  beads in a variety of
  sizes
12-inch length of
  ⅛-inch-wide ribbon
1-inch-wide ribbon

pretzel
stick
basket

Here's a great gift for the host of a bowl-game bash: a basketful of pretzel sticks and a side of gourmet mustard for dipping.

TO MAKE THE RECIPE...

soft 'n' chewy pretzel sticks

- 1 16-ounce loaf frozen white or whole wheat bread dough, thawed
- 2 tablespoons salt
- 3 quarts boiling water
- 1 egg white, slightly beaten
- 1 tablespoon water
  Coarse salt
  Sesame seed, poppy seed, dried dillweed, or coarsely ground pepper

Not all pretzels go crunch! These soft, chewy delights are more like breadsticks than crackers, and they make great dippers for a jar of flavored mustard.

1 Lightly grease 2 large baking sheets; set aside.

2 On a lightly floured surface, roll thawed dough into a 12×8-inch rectangle, occasionally stopping and letting dough rest, if necessary. Cut into twenty-four 4×1-inch strips.

3 Carefully place strips on prepared baking sheets. Bake in a 475° oven for 4 minutes. Remove from oven. Lower oven temperature to 350°.

4 In a Dutch oven or kettle dissolve the 2 tablespoons salt in the boiling water. Lower a few strips into boiling water. Boil for 2 minutes, turning once. Using a slotted spoon, remove from water and drain on paper towels. Let stand a few seconds. Place about ½ inch apart on the well-greased baking sheets.

5 In a small mixing bowl stir together egg white and 1 tablespoon water. Brush strips with some of the egg white mixture. Sprinkle strips lightly with coarse salt. Then sprinkle with sesame seed, poppy seed, dillweed, or coarsely ground pepper.

6 Bake in a 350° oven about 15 minutes or until golden brown. Immediately remove from cookie sheets and cool on wire racks. Store in an airtight container in the freezer for up to 3 months.

7 To serve (or give as gift), thaw 2 hours at room temperature or wrap in foil and heat in a 350° oven for 5 to 10 minutes until warm. Makes 24 pretzel sticks.

TO PRESENT THIS GIFT...

Tie the wide ribbon around the center of the basket, tying the ends into a bow. Tie the narrow ribbon above the wide one, knotting the ends. Tie the ends around the mustard jar, just below the lid. Knot, then tie the ends into a bow.

For the tag, cut two small rectangles from paper, one slightly smaller. Glue the paper pieces together, centering the small over the larger piece. Let glue dry. Cut small pieces of rickrack to frame the small piece of paper. Glue in place. Let glue dry. Use a paper punch to add a hole to one corner. Thread with ribbon to attach to gift.

also try this...

For another option, choose a colorful ceramic vessel to hold the pretzel sticks.

To present this gift you will need:
Wide and narrow ribbon
Tall colored basket
Small jar of gourmet mustard
Scissors
Two colors of paper
Glue stick
Rickrack
Paper punch

festive
gingerbread
loaves

Punch up the presentation of these quick lemon-topped loaves with bright paper plates trimmed with a paper punch and decorative-edge scissors.

gingerbread loaves

The orange and yellow plates add seasonal appeal to this loaf that brims with some of fall's favorite flavors.

1½ cups all-purpose flour
1 teaspoon baking powder
1 teaspoon ground cinnamon
½ teaspoon ground ginger
¼ teaspoon baking soda
¼ teaspoon salt
1 beaten egg
⅓ cup mild-flavored molasses
⅓ cup cooking oil
¼ cup packed brown sugar
¼ cup milk
1 recipe Lemon Icing
Chopped crystallized ginger (optional)
Lemon slice twists (optional)

1 Grease bottoms and halfway up the sides of two 5¾×3×2-inch individual loaf pans; set aside.

2 In a medium mixing bowl combine flour, baking powder, cinnamon, ginger, baking soda, and salt. Make a well in center of flour mixture; set aside. In another medium mixing bowl stir together egg, molasses, oil, brown sugar, and milk. Add egg mixture all at once to the flour mixture. Stir just until moistened (batter will be a little lumpy). Spoon batter into the prepared pans, dividing evenly.

3 Bake in a 350° oven for 25 to 30 minutes or until a wooden toothpick inserted near the centers comes out clean. Cool in pans on wire racks for 10 minutes. Remove from pans. Cool completely on wire racks. Wrap tightly and store in the refrigerator for up to 3 days or in the freezer for up to 1 month.

4 To present, drizzle tops of loaves with Lemon Icing. Decorate with crystallized ginger and a lemon slice twist, if desired. Makes 2 loaves.

Lemon Icing: In a small mixing bowl stir together 1 cup sifted powdered sugar and 1 teaspoon lemon juice or vanilla. Stir in milk, 1 teaspoon at a time, until icing is of drizzling consistency.

Using the photograph for inspiration, trim the edges of the paper plates, making each a different size. To add small holes around the edge, use a paper punch. Layer the plates for a colorful display.

For the tag, cut a 2×6-inch strip from craft paper. Fold in half with the short ends together. Cut narrow strips from colored papers. Glue horizontally on one side of the craft paper tag. Let the glue dry. Punch a hole in the center near the fold. Thread with ribbon.

also try this...

Use seasonally themed paper plates to present loaves around particular holidays.

To present this gift you will need:
Decorative-edge scissors
Paper plates in desired colors
Paper punch
Brown craft paper
Scissors
Colored papers to coordinate with plate colors
Glue stick
⅛-inch-wide satin ribbon

snack in a sack

A felt-trimmed shopping bag makes a clever **pouch** for something truly sweet and irresistible: homemade caramel corn.

caramel-nut corn

12 cups popped popcorn
(about ½ to ⅔ cups
unpopped)
Nonstick cooking
spray
1½ cups mixed salted
nuts
1 cup packed brown
sugar
¾ cup butter
½ cup dark-colored corn
syrup
½ teaspoon sifted
baking soda

Here's the best caramel corn we've ever tasted. You had better make a batch for yourself, or your gift bag might end up half-full!

1 Remove all unpopped kernels from popcorn. Lightly coat a roasting pan with nonstick cooking spray. Remove unpopped kernels from popped corn. Combine popcorn and nuts in the prepared pan; keep warm in 300° oven.

2 In a 2-quart saucepan combine brown sugar, butter, and corn syrup. Bring to boiling over medium heat, stirring constantly (about 12 minutes). Cook and stir for 5 minutes more. Remove from heat; stir in baking soda (the mixture will foam).

3 Pour caramel mixture over popcorn-nut mixture in prepared pan; stir gently to coat.

4 Bake in a 300° oven for 15 minutes. Stir popcorn mixture. Bake for 5 minutes more. Remove from oven. Spread on a large piece of foil to cool. Break apart to serve. Store in an airtight container at room temperature for up to 1 week. Makes about 15 cups mixture.

TO PRESENT THIS GIFT... Using gold felt for the base color, cut a rectangle ¼ inch smaller than the bag front. Trim the bottom to a point. Cut the second felt color (blue) ½ inch smaller than the base color. Cut a diamond shape from the remaining piece of felt. Layer felt shapes and sew in the center. Glue around the edges, leaving the top of the blue felt shape open like a pocket. Sew a button to the center of the felt pieces and at the point. Glue onto the bag front. Cut a length of cord to fit around the bottom button, leaving 2-inch tails. Slip tails through a pony bead. Wrap the handles with suede cord, gluing the ends to secure. Use a paper clip to hold each end in place until the glue dries. Remove paper clips. Line bag with parchment paper, waxed paper, or plastic wrap.

also try this...
Use heavy colored paper instead of felt to embellish the bag.

To present this gift you will need:
Felt in 3 colors
Pinking shears
Thread
Needle
Thick white crafts glue
2 large buttons
Brown gift bag with
  handles
Suede cord in
  3 colors
Pony bead
4 large paper clips
Parchment paper,
  waxed paper, or
  plastic wrap

playful pumpkin

There's nothing tricky about this treat. It's as simple as whipping together a fluffy cheese spread, placing it in a bowl, and threading a pumpkin with a plaid ribbon.

TO MAKE THE RECIPE...

pumpkin cream cheese

This autumn-flavored spread tastes great on bagels and other savory breads.

- 2 8-ounce packages cream cheese, softened
- 1 cup canned pumpkin
- 1/3 cup sugar
- 1 1/2 teaspoons pumpkin pie spice
- 1 teaspoon vanilla
- Freshly grated nutmeg (optional)

1 In a large mixing bowl beat cream cheese, pumpkin, sugar, pumpkin pie spice, and vanilla with an electric mixer until smooth. Transfer to a bowl. Store tightly covered in the refrigerator for up to 1 week.

2 If desired, sprinkle with a little freshly grated nutmeg before giving as a gift. Makes about 3 cups spread.

TO PRESENT THIS GIFT... Cut the top off the pumpkin, leaving an opening slightly smaller than the rim of the bowl. Scoop out the insides with a spoon. Use a hand drill to make holes around the rim, approximately 1 1/2 inches from the top edge. Twist together the wires at one end of the ribbon. Weave ribbon through drilled holes. Knot ends together. Trim ribbon ends, if needed. Place bowl in pumpkin and fill with cream cheese.

also try this...

Instead of drilling the holes, attach the ribbon with gold-colored thumbtacks.

To present this gift you will need:

Knife
Small, fresh pumpkin
Spoon
Hand drill
Wire-edge ribbon
Small clear glass bowl

apple orchard delight

The flavors of fall are captured in these autumn-inspired cookies. Give them the kaffeeklatsch treatment with ribbons, buttons, and a cute plate-and-cup snack set.

½ cup butter or margarine
⅔ cup granulated sugar
⅔ cup packed brown sugar
1 teaspoon ground cinnamon
½ teaspoon baking soda
½ teaspoon ground nutmeg
⅛ teaspoon ground cloves
1 egg
2 tablespoons milk
2 cups all-purpose flour
1 cup finely chopped apple
1 cup chopped walnuts

apple spice drops

When apple season rolls around, bake and freeze a few batches of these cookies. That way, you will have a food gift on hand all autumn long.

1 In a large mixing bowl beat butter or margarine with an electric mixer on medium to high speed for 30 seconds. Add granulated sugar, brown sugar, cinnamon, baking soda, nutmeg, and cloves; beat until combined. Beat in egg and milk. Beat in as much of the flour as you can with the mixer. Stir in any remaining flour, the apple, and the nuts with a wooden spoon. Drop dough by rounded teaspoons 2 inches apart on a lightly greased cookie sheet.

2 Bake in a 375° oven for 9 to 11 minutes or until edges are light brown. Cool on cookie sheet for 1 minute. Transfer cookies to wire racks to cool. Store cookies in a tightly covered container at room temperature for up to 3 days or in the freezer for up to 3 months. Makes about 40 cookies.

TO PRESENT THIS GIFT... Thread the ribbon through the shank hole of the button. Tie the button to the top of the cup handle. Tie the ribbon ends into a bow. Trim the ends, if needed.

also try this...

Wash and dry the glassware. Avoid touching the areas to be painted. Add polka dots to the outside of the cup by dipping a round pencil eraser into glass paint and dotting onto the outside cup surface and/or the bottom of the plate. Let it dry. Bake the painted glassware in the oven if instructed by the paint manufacturer. Let cool.

To present this gift you will need:
Thin green ribbon
Apple shank button
Glass snack cup and plate set
Scissors

berry-
bright
relish

This lovely condiment makes a perfect gift for the hosts of a Thanksgiving celebration. They'll love it first as a decoration for the holiday table and later served on leftover turkey sandwiches!

TO MAKE THE RECIPE...

gingerberry relish

1 8¼-ounce can
crushed pineapple
(syrup pack)
⅔ cup sugar
½ cup water
¾ teaspoon ground
ginger
1 12-ounce package
(3 cups) cranberries
½ cup chopped walnuts

Hold off on adding the walnuts until right before giving the gift. They're best added just before serving.

1 In a medium saucepan combine the undrained pineapple, sugar, water, and ginger. Cook and stir over medium heat until sugar is dissolved.

2 Add cranberries. Bring to boiling; reduce heat. Cook and stir 3 to 4 minutes more or until cranberries pop. Transfer to an airtight container. Cover and chill for up to 3 days. Stir in walnuts before serving. Makes 10 to 12 servings.

TO PRESENT THIS GIFT... Cut a 16-inch piece of wire. Wind one end around an ice pick so beads won't slip off. Remove the ice pick. String on 3 inches of beads, spacing glass and seed beads with gold beads. Add 8 inches of seed beads, stringing on in a pattern, if desired. Finish the end in the same manner as the first 3 inches. Wind the end of the wire around the ice pick to curl. Remove ice pick. Wrap the beaded wire around the top of the jar and twist to secure. If the wire slips down on the jar, use silicone glue to hold it in place. Let glue dry. Fill jar with Gingerberry Relish.

also try this...

Combine three colors of curling ribbon and tie them around the top of the jar. Curl the ends.

**To present
this gift you
will need:**
Wire cutters
Medium-weight
crafting wire
Ice pick
Glass beads in various
sizes and shapes
Seed beads
Small gold beads
Glass jar with lid
Silicone glue (if
needed)

bread and
butter warmth

When the cold wind starts to blow, **nestle this anything-but-ordinary spread inside a terra-cotta loaf pan for a gift that's sure to warm hearts.**

TO MAKE THE RECIPE...

sweet potato-banana butter

2 pounds sweet potatoes (about 4 medium)
2 medium, ripe bananas, cut up
1¼ cups packed brown sugar
⅔ cup honey
2 tablespoons lemon juice
1 teaspoon ground cinnamon
½ teaspoon salt
½ teaspoon ground ginger
¼ teaspoon ground nutmeg

Though sweet potatoes are available year-round, their peak seasons are autumn and winter. Conveniently, that's when this autumn-spiced spread will really hit the spot.

1 Peel sweet potatoes. Cut off woody portions and ends. Cut into quarters. Cook, covered, in enough boiling salted water to cover for 15 to 20 minutes or until tender; drain. Cool slightly.

2 Place drained sweet potatoes in a food processor bowl. Cover and process until smooth. Add the bananas; cover and process until smooth.

3 In a large saucepan stir together the sweet potato-banana mixture,

brown sugar, honey, lemon juice, cinnamon, salt, ginger, and nutmeg. Bring to boiling; reduce heat. Cook, uncovered, over very low heat about 30 minutes or until very thick, stirring frequently.

4 Place the saucepan in a sink filled with ice water to cool the sweet potato mixture. Spoon cooled mixture into storage containers. Cover and store in the refrigerator for up to 3 weeks. Makes about 4 half-pints butter.

TO PRESENT THIS GIFT... Fill glass canning jar and wipe the outside of the jar clean. Place a paper napkin over the lid. Screw on the lid and trim napkin evenly around ring with pinking shears. Fill the loaf pan with shredded paper. Nestle the jar in the pan.

also try this...
If you don't have decorative napkins on hand, use colored marking pens to add small dots to a plain white napkin.

To present this gift you will need:
Glass canning jar
Decorative paper napkin
Pinking shears
Small terra-cotta bread loaf pan
Shredded paper

great balls of fun

Popcorn balls are timeless (and seasonless) treats.
With the right colors of candies and decorations, you can design these playful goodies to go with any occasion.

20	cups popped popcorn
1½	cups light-colored corn syrup
1½	cups sugar
1	7-ounce jar marshmallow creme
2	tablespoons butter
1	teaspoon vanilla
1½	cups candy-coated milk chocolate pieces or candy-coated peanut butter-flavored pieces

popcorn and candy balls

If you wish, add a few drops of food coloring to the marshmallow mixture to further imbue these treats with seasonal hues.

1 Remove all unpopped kernels from popped popcorn. Place popcorn in a buttered 17×12×2-inch baking pan or roasting pan. Keep popcorn warm in a 300° oven while preparing marshmallow mixture.

2 In a large saucepan bring corn syrup and sugar to boiling over medium-high heat, stirring constantly. Remove from heat. Stir in marshmallow creme, butter, and vanilla until combined.

3 Pour marshmallow mixture over hot popcorn; stir gently to coat. Cool until popcorn mixture can be handled easily. Stir in candies. With damp hands, quickly shape mixture into 3-inch-diameter balls. Wrap each popcorn ball in plastic wrap. Store at room temperature up to 1 week. Makes 24 popcorn balls.

Popcorn Cake: Turn popcorn mixture into a buttered 10-inch tube pan. Press gently into pan with spatula or damp hands. Let stand about 30 minutes; remove and slice like cake.

Wash and dry the bowl. Avoid touching the areas to be painted. Paint "Halloween" around the rim of the bowl, drawing pumpkins for the Os and between each word as desired. Let dry. Bake the painted glassware in oven if instructed by the paint manufacturer. Let cool.

also try this...

Use Halloween stickers in place of painted jack-o'-lanterns.

To present this gift you will need:
White glass bowl with lip
Glass paint pens in black, orange, green, and silver

teatime tortes

A little like a tea sandwich, **a lot like a cake, these sweet treats are reason enough to linger over a cup of tea with an old friend.**

TO MAKE THE RECIPE...

½ of an 8-ounce tub cream cheese with pineapple
¼ cup butter, softened
3 tablespoons powdered sugar
½ teaspoon ground cinnamon
¼ cup finely shredded carrot
1 tablespoon finely chopped crystallized ginger
1 10¾-ounce frozen pound cake, thawed
3 tablespoons apricot preserves
   Chopped crystallized ginger (optional)

sweet cheese tortes

If you wish, present this fruit-and-cheese-stuffed torte with one of the gourmet tea blends available today.

1 In a medium mixing bowl combine cream cheese, butter, powdered sugar, and cinnamon. Beat with an electric mixer on medium speed about 30 seconds or until combined. Stir in carrot and the 1 tablespoon crystallized ginger.

2 Trim the crust from the thawed cake. Cut the cake in half crosswise; cut each half horizontally into thirds. Spread the cream cheese mixture over 3 of the 6 slices of cake. Place remaining cake slices on top. Cover and chill for 3 to 24 hours.

3 Cut up any large pieces of preserves; melt preserves in a small saucepan over low heat, stirring constantly. Uncover the 3 tortes and brush the tops of each with some of the apricot preserves. Place each torte on a small serving plate. Cut each torte in half; then cut in half again, forming four squares. Cut each square in half diagonally, forming eight small triangles per torte. If desired, top each torte triangle with chopped crystallized ginger. Store, covered, in the refrigerator for up to 24 hours. Makes 3 tortes.

TO PRESENT THIS GIFT... Cut a square piece of paper the approximate size of your glass plate. Fold the paper in half. Fold again, bringing the short sides together to form a square. Fold in half to form a triangle, making sure the folded edges meet. Holding the folded point, cut the opposite end into a point. Unfold the paper and iron between press cloths, if desired. Place on plate and arrange tortes on top of paper.

also try this...

During the winter months, cut a large snowflake from art paper or vellum to use as a plate liner.

To present this gift you will need:
White rice paper, white art paper, or vellum
Pinking shears
Iron (optional)
Press cloths (optional)
Square glass plate

silly snowmen

When it's a smile you're after, "ice" up a plate of these incognito snowmen (they're actually purchased cookies in colorful disguise).

1 cup sifted powdered sugar
¼ teaspoon vanilla
3 to 4 teaspoons milk
15 peanut-shaped peanut butter sandwich cookies
15 large gumdrops
Granulated sugar
Candy decorations or decorator icing

peanut snowmen

Keep the oven off and the mixer covered! These quick cookies begin with a favorite purchased treat and end with candy decorations. Just one step comes between start and finish: a simple icing.

1 For icing, in a small bowl combine powdered sugar, vanilla, and enough milk to make a thin icing consistency. Spread about 1 teaspoon icing over the top and sides of each peanut butter cookie so that the texture of the cookie shows through.

2 To make gumdrop hats, roll a large gumdrop into an oval in granulated sugar. Roll oval into a cone shape; press to seal ends. Curl up bottom edge of cone to form a brim. Attach hat to head of peanut butter snowman with icing. Add candy decorations or decorator icing to make dots for eyes and buttons. Store in a tightly covered container in the refrigerator for up to 3 days. Makes 15 snowmen.

Tear the fabric into squares slightly smaller than the larger plate. Trim threads, if needed. Arrange the fabric squares on the larger plate, placing so that each corner shows. Place the smaller plate on top. Arrange cookies on smaller plate.

also try this...

Use two or three coordinating paper napkins between the plates.

To present this gift you will need:
Fabric scraps
2 clear glass plates in 2 sizes
Scissors

wintertime
wonders

A simple drinking straw transforms cookies into sweet, one-of-a-kind snowflakes. A glittery snowflake-dusted box echoes the wintry motif.

citrus snowflakes

½	cup butter, softened
⅓	cup shortening
1	cup granulated sugar
⅓	cup dairy sour cream
1	egg
1	teaspoon vanilla
2	teaspoons finely shredded lemon peel (optional)
½	teaspoon finely shredded lime peel (optional)
¾	teaspoon baking powder
¼	teaspoon baking soda
	Dash salt
2½	cups all-purpose flour
	Pearl sugar, fine sanding sugar, coarse sugar, and/or white edible glitter
	Sifted powdered sugar (optional)

No two snowflakes are alike, and the same goes for these citrus-infused sweets.

1 In a large mixing bowl beat butter and shortening with an electric mixer on medium to high speed for 30 seconds. Add granulated sugar, sour cream, egg, vanilla, lemon and lime peels (if using), baking powder, baking soda, and salt. Beat until combined, scraping sides of bowl occasionally. Beat in as much of the flour as you can with the mixer. Stir in any remaining flour with a wooden spoon. Divide dough in half. Cover and chill about 2 hours or until easy to handle.

2 On a lightly floured surface, roll half of the dough at a time to ⅛- to ¼-inch thickness. Use assorted snowflake cookie cutters or a sharp knife dipped in flour to cut dough into snowflake designs. Use hors d'oeuvre cutters or straws to cut random holes in the cutout shapes so

they resemble snowflakes. Use a straw to cut half-circles from the edges to flute them. Using a wide spatula, place cookies about 1 inch apart on an ungreased cookie sheet. Sprinkle with various sugars or glitter, if desired.

3 Bake in a 375° oven for 7 to 8 minutes or until edges are firm and bottoms are very light brown. Transfer cookies to a wire rack to cool. If desired, when cookies are cool, sprinkle with powdered sugar. Store in a tightly covered container at room temperature for up to 3 days or in the freezer for up to 3 months. Makes about forty 2½-inch snowflake cookies.

To draw the snowflakes on the box, using the paint pen, first make an X, then add a third horizontal line through the X, making a basic snowflake shape. Add tiny lines or dots onto each line. Draw snowflakes on the entire box lid top and sides. Paint small random dots between the snowflakes. While the paint is still wet, sprinkle white glitter onto the painted motifs. Let dry. Line box and cover cookies with cellophane.

also try this...

Use this same technique on a solid-color cookie tin to make another special presentation for your sweet treats.

To present this gift you will need:
White paint pen
Small white box, approximately 8×8 inches
White glitter
Cellophane

cold
weather
comfort

Add sweetness and warmth to a friend's wintry day with a nostalgic milk bottle filled with chocolaty mint cocoa.

TO MAKE THE RECIPE...

²/₃ cup sugar
¹/₃ cup unsweetened cocoa powder
1¹/₃ cups nonfat dry milk powder
1 10-ounce package (1²/₃ cups) mint-flavored semisweet chocolate pieces

minty hot cocoa mix

If you can't find milk bottles, you can use any pretty 2-cup jars or bottles for this mix.

1 Layer sugar, cocoa powder, milk powder, and chocolate pieces in two 2-cup milk bottles or jars, dividing equally. Add additional chocolate pieces to bottles or jars to fill small gaps, if necessary. Tightly cover and store in a cool, dry place for up to 6 weeks. Makes 2 jars mix.

TO PRESENT THIS GIFT... First place the cocoa mix in the bottle according to the directions, above. Tie a ribbon around a candy cane for extra embellishment. Trim the ribbon ends, if needed. Include preparation directions, right, with gift.

also try this...

Use ribbon to tie a decorative stirring spoon to the neck of the milk bottle.

To present this gift you will need:
Milk bottle (available in antiques stores and at flea markets)
Ribbon
Candy cane
Scissors

PREPARATION DIRECTIONS

In a large saucepan combine contents of jar with 1²/₃ cups water. Heat and stir over medium heat until hot and chocolate pieces have melted. Pour into 4 mugs and serve with peppermint sticks or candy canes, if desired.

Fruited Vinegar,
page 151

merry
gifts for
christmas

shimmering
chocolate box

A golden box, complete with sparkling ornament and elegant ribbon, hints at the richness of the chocolate candies inside.

orange-cappuccino creams

These mocha-orange treats are indeed elegant. The great thing is that they're surprisingly easy to make, too.

1½ pounds white chocolate, chopped
½ cup whipping cream
1 tablespoon finely shredded orange peel
1 tablespoon orange liqueur or orange juice
1 teaspoon orange extract
½ cup finely chopped walnuts
About 72 small foil candy cups (1¼- to 1½-inch size)
¼ cup whipping cream
4 teaspoons instant espresso coffee powder or instant coffee crystals
8 ounces semisweet chocolate
White chocolate curls (optional)
Orange peel (optional)

1 For filling, in a large saucepan combine white chocolate, the ½ cup whipping cream, the orange peel, orange liqueur or juice, and orange extract. Stir over low heat until white chocolate is just melted. Remove from heat and stir in walnuts. Cool slightly.

2 Place mixture in a self-sealing heavy plastic bag. Using scissors, make a small opening at one bottom corner of the bag. Squeeze mixture through hole in bag to fill candy cups about two-thirds full. (Or use a small spoon instead of bag to fill cups.) Chill in the refrigerator for 20 minutes.

3 In a medium saucepan heat the ¼ cup whipping cream and the espresso powder or coffee crystals over low heat until dissolved. Add semisweet chocolate, stirring over low heat for 3 to 4 minutes or until chocolate melts. Spoon ½ teaspoon of the semisweet chocolate mixture onto each white chocolate cream. If desired, top with white chocolate curls and/or orange peel. Store in the refrigerator for up to 3 days. Serve at room temperature. Makes about 72 candies.

In a well-ventilated work area, spray-paint the outside of the lid and box bottom with gold paint. Let dry. Tie a generous ribbon bow. Attach ornament to the center of the bow. Hot-glue the bow to the center of the box lid. Let dry. Line box and cover chocolates with plastic wrap to protect them from coming into contact with the paint.

also try this...

To make a patterned background on the box, lightly sponge metallic silver acrylic paint over the gold spray paint.

To present this gift you will need:
Gold spray paint
Small, square cardboard jewelry box
Ribbon
Orange holiday ornament
Hot-glue gun and hot-glue sticks
Plastic wrap

tutti-frutti cookie tin

These festive old-world treats **deserve an equally festive cookie tin. Decoupage and colored ribbon do the trick.**

panforte bars

A little like fruitcake, panforte is an Italian pastry that's dense with nuts and candied fruit. These rich bars resemble the traditional treat in all ways except one: They're much easier to make!

1 18-ounce roll refrigerated sugar cookie dough
1 10- to 12-ounce can unsalted mixed nuts, coarsely chopped
½ cup butterscotch-flavored pieces or semisweet chocolate pieces
½ cup mixed dried fruit bits, coarsely chopped dried apricots, or golden raisins (optional)
½ cup shredded coconut

1 Lightly grease a 9x9x2-inch baking pan; set aside.

2 In a large mixing bowl stir sugar cookie dough with a wooden spoon until soft. Add nuts, butterscotch or chocolate pieces, and, if using, dried fruit. Stir until well mixed. Pat dough evenly into the prepared pan. Sprinkle coconut over top, pressing in lightly.

3 Bake in a 350° oven about 30 minutes or until a wooden toothpick inserted near center comes out clean. Cool completely in pan on a wire rack. Cut into bars. Store in a tightly covered container at room temperature for up to 3 days or in the freezer for up to 3 months. Makes about 32 bars.

In a well-ventilated work area, spray-paint the lid and the base of the tin. Let it dry. Cut lengths of ribbon to fit the lid of the tin. Using decoupage medium, decoupage strips of colored ribbon onto the lid. Repeat with the base of the tin. To decoupage, apply medium to tin, lay down ribbon, and paint entire surface of tin and ribbon with more decoupage medium. Let it dry. Hot-glue an ornament in the center of the lid. Let it dry. Line box and cover bars with parchment paper or waxed paper to protect food from coming into contact with painted and decoupaged surfaces.

also try this...

Decoupage tins with other holiday-themed items, such as recycled holiday postage stamps, wrapping paper, and holiday newspaper clippings.

To present this gift you will need:
Deep red spray paint
Round food tin
Scissors
Colored ribbon
Decoupage medium
Paintbrush
Hot-glue gun and hot-glue sticks
Holiday ornament
Parchment paper or waxed paper

a bag of
biscotti

Slice your way to an easy yet special gift **with slice-and-bake cookies and a few well-placed slits in a paper bag.**

christmas biscotti

These twice-baked treats make marvelous dunkers. Present them with a bag of gourmet coffee beans for a perfectly paired gift.

2/3 cup Vanilla Sugar (see recipe, page 15)
1/3 cup butter
2 teaspoons baking powder
1/2 teaspoon ground cardamom
2 eggs
2 cups all-purpose flour
3/4 cup dried cranberries or snipped dried cherries
3/4 cup chopped, shelled green pistachio nuts

1 Prepare the Vanilla Sugar. In a mixer bowl beat butter with an electric mixer on medium speed for 30 seconds. Add the 2/3 cup Vanilla Sugar, the baking powder, and cardamom; beat until combined. Beat in the eggs. Beat in as much of the flour as you can with the mixer. Stir in any remaining flour and the cranberries or cherries and pistachio nuts until combined. Divide dough in half. If necessary, cover and chill dough until easy to handle.

2 Shape each portion of dough into a 9-inch roll. Place 4 inches apart on a lightly greased cookie sheet, flattening slightly until 2 inches wide.

3 Bake in a 375° oven for 25 to 30 minutes or until a wooden toothpick inserted near the center comes out clean. Cool loaves on the cookie sheet for 1 hour.

4 Cut each loaf diagonally into 1/2-inch slices using a serrated knife. Place slices, cut sides down, on an ungreased cookie sheet. Bake in a 325° oven for 8 minutes. Turn slices over; bake 8 to 10 minutes more or until dry and crisp. Transfer to a wire rack to cool. Store in a tightly covered container at room temperature for up to 3 days or in the freezer for up to 3 months. Makes about 32 biscotti.

To make a tree pattern, fold the piece of printer paper in half. Using the fold as the tree center, cut a simple tree shape, smaller than the front of the paper bag. Open the pattern and place it in the center of the bag. Trace around the pattern on the front of the sack, tracing only the right side. Place cardboard in sack. Using a crafts knife, cut along line and fold back. Cut a whole tree shape from another bag. Paint one side silver; let dry. Fold in half. Glue fold to center of tree on bag. Glue silver paper behind opening. Let glue dry. Draw a horizontal 1×3-inch rectangle at the tree base. Color in with gold marker. Cut out three 1/4×1-inch pieces from extra bag. Glue pieces vertically on gold rectangle as shown in picture. Let glue dry. Outline the outside edge of the tree shape using a gold marker. Add star stickers where desired. Line bag with parchment paper or waxed paper.

also try this...

For quick cutout shapes, use a symmetrical cookie cutter such as a bell, angel, or snowman.

To present this gift you will need:
Printer paper
Scissors
Pencil
2 brown lunch sacks
Cardboard
Crafts knife
Paintbrush
Silver paint
Thick white crafts glue
Gold marker
Star stickers
Parchment paper or waxed paper

tree-topped treats

A favorite holiday candy **gets all decked out in a box topped with a trio of merry Christmas trees.**

TO MAKE THE RECIPE...

1 pound vanilla-flavored candy coating, cut up
¾ cup finely crushed red and/or green striped round peppermint candies
Red food coloring (optional)
⅓ cup semisweet chocolate pieces

marbled mint bark

Get the kids involved in the holiday cooking spirit. This recipe is easy enough for them to make, and a perfect gift for giving to friends or teachers.

1 Line a baking sheet with foil; set aside.

2 Microwave candy coating in a microwave-safe 4-cup glass measure on 100% power (high) for 2 to 3 minutes, stirring after every minute. Stir in crushed candies and, if desired, red food coloring to tint to desired color. Pour coating mixture onto prepared baking sheet to about ¼-inch thickness.

3 Microwave chocolate pieces in a glass measure on high for 1 to 2 minutes or until soft enough to stir smooth, stirring after 1 minute. Drizzle over peppermint mixture. Gently zigzag a narrow metal spatula through the chocolate and peppermint layer to marble.

4 Let candy stand several hours or until firm. Or chill about 30 minutes or until firm. Use foil to lift candy from baking sheet; carefully break candy into pieces. Store, tightly covered, at room temperature for up to 2 weeks. Makes about 1¼ pounds candy.

TO PRESENT THIS GIFT...

Arrange and glue bottlebrush trees in a cluster in the center of the box lid. Let the glue dry. Paint the stars yellow. Let dry. Glue a star to the top of each tree. Let dry. Tie raffia below each star. Trim the ends. Line box with tissue paper, waxed paper, or parchment paper.

also try this...

Use small, lightweight plastic holiday figurines to embellish the box lid.

To present this gift you will need:
Thick white crafts glue
3 small bottlebrush trees or other 4- to 6-inch artificial trees
Clean white box with lid
Paintbrush
Yellow paint
Wood star shapes
Red raffia
Scissors
Tissue paper, waxed paper, or parchment paper

glittering tidbits

Let these fairy-dusted cookie tidbits, decked with a garland of Christmasy beads, work a little magic this season.

elfin shortbread bites

1¼ cups all-purpose flour
3 tablespoons sugar
½ cup butter
2 tablespoons colored sprinkles

Maybe elves do exist! It certainly is a wonder when flour, butter, and sugar are so easily transformed into home-baked magic.

1 In a medium mixing bowl stir together flour and sugar. Using a pastry blender, cut in butter until mixture resembles fine crumbs and starts to cling. Stir in sprinkles. Form mixture into a ball and knead until smooth.

2 Roll or pat dough on an ungreased cookie sheet into an 8×5-inch rectangle. Cut into ½-inch squares. Separate the squares on the cookie sheet.

3 Bake in a 325° oven for 12 to 14 minutes or until the bottoms just start to brown. Transfer to wire racks covered with waxed paper to cool. Store in a tightly covered container at room temperature for up to 3 days or in the freezer for up to 3 months. Makes about 160 tiny cookies.

TO PRESENT THIS GIFT... Punch holes on opposite sides of the cone, just below the rim. Punch another hole in the tip. Cut a length of beaded wire for the handle. Thread bead ends through punched holes, twisting ends to secure. Make a small tassel out of a 16-inch length of beads, wrapping into 2-inch-long loops. Tie at the top with another piece of beaded wire. Tie onto the cone through the punched hole in the cone's tip.

also try this...

Use cone-shape paper drinking cups in the same way, decorating the outside with stickers in desired colors and shapes.

To present this gift you will need:
Paper punch
Flexible plastic cone (available in the doll-making supply area of crafts stores)
Scissors
Colored beaded wire

candy-wrapped nut goodies

Sugar-roasted nuts always disappear in a hurry. Fortunately, a pretty cut-glass container makes a lasting souvenir of your thoughtful gift.

TO MAKE THE RECIPE...

4   cups whole
    unblanched almonds
    or mixed nuts
1   egg white
1   teaspoon water
⅓   cup granulated sugar
⅓   cup packed brown
    sugar
2   teaspoons ground
    cinnamon
½   teaspoon salt

sugar-roasted almonds

The cinnamon flavor is meant to stand out in these sugary almonds, so be sure the cinnamon you use is a fresh, premium brand.

1 Spread almonds or mixed nuts in a single layer in a shallow baking pan. Bake in a 350° oven for 10 minutes. Remove from oven; let stand to cool (about 30 minutes).

2 In a large mixing bowl beat egg white and water with a wire whisk or rotary beater until frothy. Stir in granulated sugar, brown sugar, cinnamon, and salt. Stir in cooled nuts. Spread nuts in a single layer in a greased 15×10×1-inch baking pan.

3 Bake in a 325° oven about 20 minutes or until nuts appear dry, stirring once halfway through baking. Spread on waxed paper, separating into individual pieces or small clusters to cool. Store in a tightly covered container in the refrigerator for up to 1 week. Makes 5½ cups nuts.

TO PRESENT THIS GIFT... Fill the dish with almonds. Cut a piece of cellophane approximately 10 inches longer than the dish. Wrap the container, taping to secure. Tie ribbon around both ends of cellophane to resemble hard candy.

also try this...

Use a Chinese-food take-out box or a cylinder-shape container in place of the cut-glass dish.

To present this gift you will need:
Cut-glass dish
Colored cellophane
Scissors
Tape
Ribbon

cupful
of cheese
bites

An easy-to-make antipasto treat **comes neatly stashed in gold-studded plastic cups wrapped in holiday ribbon.**

fresh mozzarella with basil

16	ounces fresh mozzarella cheese
¼	cup roasted garlic oil or olive oil
2	teaspoons balsamic vinegar
2	tablespoons snipped fresh basil or 1 teaspoon dried basil, crushed
1	tablespoon dried whole mixed peppercorns, cracked

Use this as a basic recipe, with the option of varying the cheese and herbs. Try feta with oregano or dill, or queso fresco with cumin or red pepper flakes. Advise the recipient to serve this appetizer with baguette slices and, if desired, tomato.

1 Cut mozzarella into 1-inch cubes and place in a medium bowl. For marinade, combine oil, vinegar, basil, and cracked peppercorns. Pour over cheese and toss gently until cheese is well coated.

2 Cover and store in the refrigerator for up to 3 days. Makes 14 to 16 servings.

TO PRESENT THIS GIFT... Dot the outside of the two paper cups with glitter glue and let dry. Make two small slits (the same width as the ribbon) opposite from each other below the rim of one cup. Make just one slit below the rim of the second cup. Place the center of the ribbon under the first cup. Bring the ribbon ends up the sides of the cup and thread them through the corresponding slits. Invert a second cup over the first and thread one ribbon up through the slit in the second cup. This will make a hinge to join one side of the container. Fill the first cup with cheese bites. Bring both ribbon ends together at the top of the cup and tie them into a bow.

also try this...

For an even quicker last-minute container, use holiday stickers instead of gold glitter glue to decorate the paper cups.

To present this gift you will need:
2 red paper cups
Gold glitter glue
Crafts knife
1 yard of gold-and-red ribbon

chock-full-of-
chocolate wreath

Let's face it—when it comes to chocolate lovers, sugar cookies just don't cut it! A merry brownie wreath, on the other hand, is all about their favorite flavor!

TO MAKE THE RECIPE...

1 19- to 22-ounce package fudge brownie mix
Purchased vanilla frosting
Green paste food coloring
Red, green, and white candies for decorating

brownie wreath

During the holiday season, keep the ingredients for this recipe on hand for last-minute school or bake-sale treats. The outer crust will soften and cut easier if you wrap and store the wreath overnight.

1 Grease and flour a 10-inch fluted tube pan; set aside.

2 Prepare brownie mix according to package directions for cake brownies; spread batter into the prepared pan.

3 Bake in a 325° oven for 40 to 45 minutes or until toothpick inserted near center of cake comes out clean. Cool in pan on wire rack for 10 minutes. Remove from pan. Cool thoroughly on rack.

4 Tint frosting with green food coloring to desired color. Decorate cake with frosting and candies. Wrap well and store in an airtight container at room temperature for up to 3 days. Makes 24 servings.

TO PRESENT THIS GIFT...

First wash and dry the plate. Place brownie wreath in the center. Cut a bow shape from red paper. Cut an oval for the bow center. Use a ring of tape to secure bow center. Personalize bow with marking pens, if desired. Place bow at the top of the brownie ring.

also try this...

Instead of a construction-paper bow, use a ribbon bow for the wreath's finishing touch.

To present this gift you will need:
Round plate
Scissors
Red construction paper
Tape
Marking pens (optional)

appetizer
elegance

This lavish Lemon-Basil Cheese Ball is so special it deserves to be put on a pedestal. And that's exactly what we suggest you do!

TO MAKE THE RECIPE...

lemon-basil cheese ball

1 8-ounce carton mascarpone cheese
1 cup shredded Gruyère cheese (4 ounces)
3 tablespoons finely chopped pistachio nuts
2 tablespoons finely snipped fresh basil
4 teaspoons finely shredded lemon peel
⅛ teaspoon pepper

Mix and shape the cheese ball up to 24 hours ahead. Just before presenting, unmold it onto the serving dish.

1 In a mixing bowl beat mascarpone with an electric mixer on medium to high speed for 30 seconds. Stir in Gruyère. Stir in pistachios, basil, lemon peel, and pepper.

2 Line a 2-cup bowl with plastic wrap. Transfer cheese mixture to bowl; cover and chill 3 hours or until firm. (Can be refrigerated up to 3 days.) To serve, unmold onto a serving plate; remove plastic wrap. Makes 24 servings.

TO PRESENT THIS GIFT...

On the cutting board, cut thin slices of lemon. Line the pedestal candle holder with parchment paper. Arrange the slices around the edge of the parchment paper. Unmold the cheese ball onto the center of the lemon ring; remove plastic wrap. Garnish with a basil sprig.

also try this...

Shop discount stores for inexpensive dishes with holiday motifs for a last-minute presentation idea.

To present this gift you will need:
Cutting board
Sharp knife
Lemon
Large pedestal candle holder
Parchment paper
Basil sprig

jolly
vinegar
jars

Tiny bells spring from the corky caps of these unique vinegar jars. Who wouldn't love a gift that's festive, fruity, and fun?

fruited vinegar

1 cup rice vinegar or white vinegar
1 bag raspberry-, orange-, blackberry-, or cranberry-flavored tea

If you have a favorite recipe for a dynamite vinaigrette that would make good use of this vinegar, share your secret and attach it to the bottle.

1 In a glass measure combine the vinegar and tea bag. Cover and chill for 2 hours. Remove tea bag. Pour into a clean glass bottle and cover with a cork or nonmetallic lid. Store in a cool, dark place for up to 6 months. Use vinegar in salad dressings and in meat marinades that call for a fruit-flavored vinegar. Makes 1 cup vinegar.

Ginger-Orange Vinegar: Add ½ teaspoon grated fresh ginger and an orange tea bag to the 1 cup vinegar. Strain vinegar before pouring into the clean bottle. Cover with a cork or nonmetallic lid.

TO PRESENT THIS GIFT... Use needle to make four holes in the cork, top to bottom, like holes in a four-hole button. Cut an 18-inch length of both colors of wire. Fold each piece of wire in half. From the bottom of the cork, push the wire ends through the holes, making an X on the bottom of the cork. Thread two silver flat beads over all wire ends. Thread each wire through a silver pony bead, then through a long, thin silver bead. On the green wires, slide on a red, then a silver bead. On the red wires, slide on a green, then a silver bead. Leaving 1 inch at the end, wrap the wire ends around an ice pick to curl; remove ice pick. Slip a jingle bell on the end of each wire. Loop the wire ends to secure the jingle bells. Thread metallic beads on a 6-inch length of wire. Thread on enough beads to go around the neck of the bottle. Twist the wire ends together to secure. Trim the excess wire.

also try this...

The beaded ring around the bottle neck can also be used as a napkin ring. Make numerous rings in this same manner and give them as a matching set.

To present this gift you will need:
Sharp needle
Bottle with cork
Wire cutters
Metallic wire in red and green
2 silver flat beads
Silver pony beads
Silver long, thin beads
Metallic beads in red, green, and silver
Ice pick
4 small silver jingle bells

cheesecake
and cheer

Personalized glassware gilded with your handwritten
holiday wishes makes a striking presentation for
this marvelous marbled cheesecake.

TO MAKE THE RECIPE...

double-chocolate swirl cheesecake

³/₄ cup finely crushed
chocolate wafers
(about 14 cookies)
3 tablespoons butter,
melted
2 8-ounce packages
cream cheese,
softened
²/₃ cup sugar
²/₃ cup dairy sour cream
2 tablespoons all-
purpose flour
1 teaspoon vanilla
2 eggs
2 ounces bittersweet or
semisweet chocolate,
melted and cooled*
3 ounces white
chocolate baking
squares, melted and
cooled*
Chocolate curls
(optional)

If you're worried that the recipients of this gift might already have
received too many sweets, don't be! This one freezes for up to a
month, so they can cherish it after all the other goodies are gone.

1 For crust, in a small mixing bowl stir
together the crushed wafers and melted
butter. Press mixture onto the bottom of
an ungreased 8-inch springform pan.
Set aside.

2 For filling, in a large mixing bowl beat
cream cheese, sugar, sour cream, flour,
and vanilla with an electric mixer on
medium speed until combined. Add eggs;
beat on low speed just until combined.
(Do not overbeat.)

3 Divide filling in half. Stir melted
bittersweet chocolate into one portion.
Pour into the crust-lined pan. Stir melted
white baking squares into remaining
portion. Carefully pour on top of
bittersweet chocolate filling. Using a
narrow metal spatula or table knife, gently
swirl fillings.

4 Place springform pan in a shallow
baking pan in oven. Bake in a 325° oven
about 40 minutes or until center appears
nearly set when shaken. (Center will

appear soft set but will become firmer as
cheesecake cools.) Remove springform
pan from baking pan. Cool cheesecake on
a wire rack for 15 minutes. Use a small
metal spatula to loosen the sides of
cheesecake from pan. Cool for
30 minutes more. Remove sides of
springform pan. Cool for 1 hour. Cover
and chill at least 4 hours.

5 If desired, using two long metal
spatulas, carefully loosen and lift
cheesecake from bottom of springform
pan. Transfer cheesecake to desired platter
or foil-covered cardboard round. Wrap
cheesecake and store in the refrigerator
for up to 3 days or freeze for up to
1 month. If desired, garnish top of
cheesecake with chocolate curls before
serving. Makes 1 cheesecake (8 servings).

*Note: For best results when melting,
it's important to place each of the
chocolates in a small heavy saucepan
over very low heat and stir just until
the chocolate is smooth.

TO PRESENT THIS GIFT... Using gold pen, write "Merry Christmas" and other holiday
greetings around the edge of the cake stand. Make a dot between
each of the sayings. Write "Noel" around the edge of the base. Write "Joy"
around the edge of the plates. Let dry. Add shadows with black pen by
outlining the letters on one side. Place a gold doily on the cake stand before
setting the cheesecake on top.

also try this...

Write the words from favorite Christmas carols around the edges
of the glassware.

**To present
this gift you
will need:**
Medium gold and
fine-line black
marking pens for
glass
Clear glass cake stand
Clear glass dessert
plates
Gold paper doily

cranberry creation

A tall bottle of cranberry syrup sparkles with one of the brightest colors and flavors of the season.

TO MAKE THE RECIPE...

- 2½ cups cranberry juice
- 1 cup cranberries
- ¾ cup light-colored corn syrup
- ¼ cup sugar

cranberry syrup

Pancakes, waffles, and even ice cream get a flavor boost with a generous pour of this sweet-tart syrup.

1 In a medium saucepan combine cranberry juice, cranberries, corn syrup, and sugar. Stir to dissolve sugar. Bring to a rolling boil over medium-high heat. Reduce heat to medium. Boil 30 to 40 minutes or until reduced to 2½ cups.

2 Pour syrup through a small-mesh strainer or a strainer lined with 100-percent-cotton cheesecloth. Discard cranberries. Cover and store syrup in the refrigerator for up to 1 week. Makes 2 cups syrup.

TO PRESENT THIS GIFT... Put on the gloves to protect your hands. Using the paintbrush, paint etching cream in a band around the bottom of the bottle, following the etching cream manufacturer's instructions. Let the bottle dry after washing off the cream. Add random dots with the paint pen to the unetched area of the bottle. Let dry. Pour Cranberry Syrup into bottle. Replace cap. Fold square of white cloth over top of bottle; secure with gold cord.

also try this...

To achieve an etched effect, use frosted spray paint, masking off areas you want to remain clear.

To present this gift you will need:

Plastic gloves
Paintbrush
Etching cream
Clear glass bottle
White paint pen
White cloth
Gold cord

merry and bright bread

Imagine the joy you'll spread **when you give away this festive bread, studded with holiday flavors and fashioned into an unmistakably Christmasy shape.**

TO MAKE THE RECIPE...

poinsettia-shape fruit bread

The sprinkling of dried fruits will bring an extra touch of holiday magic.

3¼ to 3¾ cups all-purpose flour
2 packages active dry yeast
¾ cup milk
⅓ cup butter or margarine
⅓ cup granulated sugar
1 teaspoon salt
2 eggs
¾ cup golden raisins
¾ cup dried cranberries
2 teaspoons finely shredded lemon peel
1 egg white, slightly beaten
1 tablespoon water
Coarse sugar

1 In a large mixing bowl combine 1½ cups of the flour and the yeast. In a medium saucepan heat and stir milk, butter, granulated sugar, and salt until warm (120° to 130°) and butter almost melts. Add milk mixture to flour mixture along with the eggs. Beat with an electric mixer on low to medium speed for 30 seconds, scraping bowl. Beat on high speed for 3 minutes. Stir in raisins, dried cranberries, lemon peel, and as much of the remaining flour as you can.

2 Turn dough out onto a lightly floured surface. Knead in enough of the remaining flour to make a moderately soft dough that is smooth and elastic (3 to 5 minutes total). Shape into a ball. Place in a lightly greased bowl; turn once. Cover and let rise in a warm place until double (1½ to 2 hours).

3 Punch dough down. Turn out onto a lightly floured surface. Divide dough into thirds. Cover; let rest for 10 minutes. Grease 3 baking sheets.

4 Roll each portion of dough into an 8-inch square. Carefully transfer one of the squares to one of the baking sheets, reshaping as necessary. Using a sharp knife, cut 4-inch slits from the corner to within ½ inch of the center of the square. Fold every other point to the center to form a pinwheel. Use water to moisten points of dough in center and press to seal. Repeat with remaining squares and baking sheets. Cover and let rise in a warm place until nearly double (about 50 minutes). Place 2 of the baking sheets, covered, in the refrigerator while the first loaf bakes.

5 Stir together egg white and water. Before baking, lightly brush mixture over loaf. Sprinkle with coarse sugar. Bake, one loaf at a time, in a 325° oven for 20 to 25 minutes or until golden. Transfer pinwheel to wire rack and let cool. Repeat with remaining baking sheets from refrigerator. (Store egg white mixture, covered, in refrigerator when not in use.) Store loaves in airtight containers at room temperature for up to 2 days or in the freezer up to 1 month. Makes 3 pinwheel loaves.

TO PRESENT THIS GIFT... Cut grape leaves into the shape of poinsettia leaves. Place fruit bread pinwheel atop grape leaves in center of clear glass plate to resemble a poinsettia flower and its leaves.

also try this...
Layer clean, dried leaves between two glass plates for a fun effect.

To present this gift you will need:
Scissors
Paper grape leaves (purchased from a cooks' catalog or specialty store)
Square clear glass plate

christmas
bread box

Homespun bread rounds **nestle inside a vintage lunch box found at an antiques store or a flea market.**

TO MAKE THE RECIPE...

1   16-ounce package hot roll mix
3/4   cup shredded Swiss cheese (3 ounces)
2   small onions, thinly sliced and separated into rings (2/3 cup)
1   tablespoon snipped fresh rosemary or 1 teaspoon dried rosemary, crushed
1   tablespoon cooking oil

rosemary and swiss buns

These buns also make a good gift for someone who's feeling under the weather. Serve them up with a packaged soup mix. The recipient will feel much better (and much loved).

1 Grease 2 large baking sheets; set aside. Prepare hot roll mix according to package directions, except stir in Swiss cheese with the liquid. Continue with package directions through the kneading and resting steps. After dough rests, divide into 12 equal portions and shape into balls.

2 On a lightly floured surface, roll each ball into a 4-inch round. Place on prepared baking sheets. Cover and set aside.

3 In a medium skillet cook and stir onions and rosemary in hot oil until onion is tender. Using your fingertips, make 1/2-inch-deep indentations on the surface of the dough rounds. Divide the onion mixture among the tops of the rounds. Cover and let rise in a warm place until nearly double (30 to 40 minutes).

4 Bake in a 375° oven for 12 to 15 minutes or until golden. Transfer buns to a wire rack and cool completely. Place in an airtight container or bag or wrap in foil. Store in the refrigerator for up to 3 days or freeze for up to 1 month. Makes 12 buns.

TO PRESENT THIS GIFT...

Simply line lunch box with cellophane. Fill with Rosemary and Swiss Buns.

also try this...
Use alphabet stickers to spell out a personalized message on the lunch box.

To present this gift you will need:
Small metal vintage lunch box
Colored cellophane

top-hatted
topping

A jar of nut topping gets its own special topper—
a hand-painted snowman dancing on the lid.

honey-nut topping

1 10-ounce can mixed
nuts (without
peanuts)
1¼ cups honey
⅓ cup maple syrup

This sweet-and-salty topping requires no cooking, and as far
as easygoing gifts go, that's hard to top!

1 In a medium mixing bowl combine
the nuts, honey, and maple syrup. Stir
until nuts are coated. Spoon nuts and
syrup mixture into 3 clean, dry half-pint
jars. Cover and store at room temperature
for up to 3 weeks. Serve over cereal,
pound cake, fresh fruit, or ice cream.
Makes 3 half-pint jars topping.

TO PRESENT THIS GIFT... In the center of the jar lid, drill a
hole large enough to
accommodate the bolt. In a well-ventilated
work area, spray-paint the outside of the
lid silver-blue. Let dry. From the bottom,
push the bolt through the hole in the
center of the lid. Place the nut on the bolt,
screwing on tightly to secure. The bolt will
be sticking out the top of the lid. Form a
small snowman, approximately 3 inches
tall, from three balls of clay. Press over the
stove bolt. To form the hat, first make a
flat brim approximately the size of a
quarter. Add the hat top. Press together
and press on top of the snowman's head.
Make a tiny carrot-shape nose from the
clay. Break a 1-inch piece off the end of a
toothpick. Press the carrot nose onto the
broken toothpick. Press the opposite end
of the toothpick into the snowman's face.

Use scissors to cut slits down the wide
ends of two toothpicks. Press into the
snowman for arms. Let the clay dry. Paint
the hat black. Paint the nose orange. Paint
the arms with a mix of white and black. To
make the eyes, mouth, and buttons, dip
the handle end of a paintbrush into paint
and dot onto the surface. Let the paint
dry. Tie a narrow ribbon around the
snowman for the scarf. Paint the
snowman with glitter glaze. Tie a generous
ribbon bow around the top of the jar. Trim
ribbon ends. Use plastic wrap to cover
topping to protect it from the spray-
painted lid.

also try this...

Decoupage snowflake confetti
to the top of a painted lid.

**To present
this gift you
will need:**
Drill and bit
2½-inch-long stove
bolt and nut
Jar with large wood lid
Silver-blue spray paint
White air-dry clay,
such as Crayola
Model Magic
Flat toothpicks
Scissors
Paintbrush
Acrylic paints in black,
orange, and white
¼-inch-wide ribbon
for scarf
Glitter glaze
1-inch-wide ribbon
Plastic wrap

baubles and bites

Surprise a friend with a glittering take-out box piled high with tasty blue cheese appetizers and a couple of holiday baubles, to boot.

TO MAKE THE RECIPE...

1½ cups all-purpose flour
2 to 3 teaspoons cracked black pepper
8 ounces blue cheese
¼ cup butter
1 cup chopped walnuts
2 egg yolks, slightly beaten

blue cheese and walnut bites

No need to provide the crackers or spreading knife with this gift! These easy-to-make nibbles offer cheese flavor and cracker crunch all in one bite!

1 In a medium mixing bowl combine flour and pepper. Using a pastry blender, cut in cheese and butter until mixture resembles coarse crumbs. Add walnuts and egg yolks. Stir until combined. Form the mixture into a ball; knead until combined.

2 Divide dough in half. Shape each half into a log about 9 inches long. If desired, flatten sides of log, making a square log. Wrap logs in plastic wrap; chill at least 2 hours.

3 Cut each log into ¼-inch slices. Place slices 1 inch apart on an ungreased baking sheet. Bake in a 425° oven for 8 to 10 minutes or until bottoms and edges are golden brown. Transfer to a wire rack. Serve warm or at room temperature. Store in a tightly covered container in the refrigerator for up to 1 week. Makes about 72 appetizers.

TO PRESENT THIS GIFT...

In a well-ventilated work area, lightly mist the container with spray paints to make flecks of gold and silver on the outside of the container. Let dry. Place gold star stickers randomly on the container. Present with plastic Christmas tree ornaments, if desired. Use parchment paper, waxed paper, or plastic wrap to line box and cover appetizers to protect them from the spray-painted surfaces.

also try this...

Draw stars on the container using metallic gold and silver marking pens.

To present this gift you will need:
Chinese take-out container in desired color
Spray paint in gold and silver
Gold star stickers
Plastic Christmas tree ornaments (optional)
Parchment paper, waxed paper, or plastic wrap

christmas-wrapped
condiment

Personalize this sweet-and-spicy condiment by covering it in a gold-tinged screen, and you'll have another terrific holiday gift all wrapped up.

TO MAKE THE RECIPE...

papaya-rum chutney

5 to 6 papayas* or
6 mangoes
4 large cloves garlic, quartered
4 large chile peppers (see note, page 25)
2 cups packed light brown sugar
1½ cups cider vinegar
½ cup light rum

For a nonalcoholic version, omit the rum, but watch the mixture closely during cooking. The cooking time will be slightly shorter.

1 Halve papayas; scoop out seeds. Peel papayas. Chop and measure 6 cups. (To prepare mangoes, make a cut through each mango, sliding a sharp knife next to the seed along one side of the mango. Repeat on other side of the seed, resulting in 2 large pieces. Cut away all of the meat that remains around the seed. Remove peel on all pieces and cut up the meat.) Place fruit in a 4- to 6-quart Dutch oven or kettle. Add garlic. Peel, seed, and chop chile peppers; measure about ½ cup and add to kettle. Add brown sugar and vinegar.

2 Heat mixture over medium heat to boiling. Reduce heat; add rum.

Boil gently, uncovered, for 30 to 40 minutes or until desired consistency, stirring occasionally.

3 Immediately ladle hot chutney into hot, sterilized half-pint canning jars, leaving ½-inch headspace. Wipe rims and adjust lids. Process the filled jars in a boiling-water canner for 10 minutes (start timing when water begins to boil). Remove the jars from the canner; cool jars on racks. Makes about 5 cups chutney.

*Note: Select papayas that are slightly firm to the touch; avoid overripe papayas for this recipe.

TO PRESENT THIS GIFT... In a well-ventilated work area, place screen on newspapers. Center cardboard on screen. Spray-paint edge of screen gold. Let dry. Turn over and repeat. Place jar in center of screen. Fold sides up. Secure at top with wire. Wrap each wire end around a pencil to curl. Remove pencil. Tuck berry sprigs in top.

also try this...
Use colored cellophane to cover jar, and secure with colored chenille stems.

To present this gift you will need:
18-inch square of silver-colored screen (available from crafts stores)
Newspapers
13-inch square of cardboard
Metallic gold spray paint
Gold wire
Pencil
Artificial berry sprigs

jewel-topped
coffee mix

Presented in a jewel-topped shaker jar, this coffee mix gives its recipients good reason to take a break during the busy holiday season. And that's a rare gift indeed!

TO MAKE THE RECIPE...

café-au-lait mix

½ cup powdered nondairy creamer
½ cup buttermints, lightly crushed
¼ cup sifted powdered sugar
2 cups nonfat dry milk powder
⅔ cup instant coffee crystals
Peppermint sticks or round hard candies (optional)

Though it's easy to make and comes together quickly, the recipients will love slowly savoring this creamy blend.

1 In a medium mixing bowl stir together nondairy creamer, buttermints, powdered sugar, and milk powder. Layer mixture with coffee crystals, dividing among two 2-cup jars. If desired, insert peppermint sticks or candies to fill jars snugly. Cover and store in a cool, dry place for up to 6 weeks. Makes 2 jars mix (1 cup each).

TO PRESENT THIS GIFT... Layer ingredients into shaker jar as directed in recipe. Trace around the lid onto the paper. Cut out slightly smaller than traced line. Place paper on lid, under the ring. Adjust lid on top of jar. If necessary, cut off the shank of the button using a wire cutter. Hot-glue the button in the center of the paper circle. Let it dry. Tie ribbons around the lid. Include preparation directions, below, with gift.

also try this...

Use a scrap of pretty fabric to cover the lid and a flea-market earring or pin for the crowning jewel.

PREPARATION DIRECTIONS

For each serving, place ¼ cup of the mix in a mug and add ⅔ cup boiling water. Stir until the mix dissolves. Serve with a peppermint stick or candy, if desired.

To present this gift you will need:
Shaker jar with ring lid
Decorative paper
Pencil
Scissors
Button
Wire cutter
Hot-glue gun and hot-glue sticks
Ribbons

crock full
of tapenade

Show your true colors as a friend this season with this richly hued French tapenade that sparkles in its clear crock.

tricolor tapenade

¼ cup pitted ripe olives
¼ cup pimiento-stuffed green olives
¼ cup purchased roasted sweet red peppers
1 teaspoon olive oil
1 teaspoon snipped fresh oregano
¼ teaspoon ground black pepper

Tapenade, a terrific olive spread that hails from the south of France, tastes *magnifique* served over toasted baguette slices.

1 In a food processor bowl combine ripe olives, green olives, sweet red peppers, olive oil, oregano, and black pepper. Cover and process with several on-off turns until coarsely chopped. (Or coarsely chop olives and sweet peppers by hand. Stir in oil, oregano, and ground black pepper.)

2 Transfer to a jar and chill, covered, before serving. Store in a tightly covered glass container in the refrigerator for up to 2 weeks. Makes about ½ cup tapenade.

Cut lengths of cord to wrap around the top and bottom of the jar base. Glue in place. Let the glue dry.

For the tag, cut a small rectangle from black paper. Use a paper punch to make random holes around the edges. Glue on top of the yellow paper, trimming to the same size as the black paper. Let glue dry. Glue on top of the red paper. Let glue dry. Trim red paper to ¼ inch from the edges of the black paper. Punch a hole in one corner. Use a metallic marker to write the name of the recipient on the tag. Tie the tag to the jar with cord.

also try this...

Wrap the jar with brightly colored shoelaces as an alternative to cord.

To present this gift you will need:
Scissors
Colored papers in black, yellow, and red
Small paper punch
Thick white crafts glue
Metallic marker
Satin cord in desired color

coffeehouse pleasures

Coffee lovers will delight in a pretty cup filled with gourmet beans and topped with chocolate-dipped spoons for stirring sweetness into their favorite brew.

coffeehouse chocolate spoons

6 ounces semisweet chocolate pieces
20 to 24 plastic spoons
6 ounces white baking bar

These chocolate-dipped spoons make it easy for anyone to stir up something sweet and indulgent in minutes.

1 In a heavy saucepan heat semisweet chocolate pieces over low heat, stirring constantly until the chocolate begins to melt. Immediately remove from heat; stir until smooth. Dip half of the spoons into chocolate, tapping handle of each spoon against side of pan to remove excess chocolate. Place spoons on waxed paper; refrigerate for 30 minutes to allow chocolate to set up.

2 In a heavy saucepan heat white baking bar over low heat, stirring constantly until baking bar begins to melt. Immediately remove from heat; stir until smooth. Dip remaining spoons into the melted baking bar. Refrigerate for 30 minutes to set up.

3 Place the remaining melted white baking bar in a small, self-sealing heavy plastic bag. Using scissors, make a small opening at one bottom corner of the bag; drizzle one or both sides of the chocolate-coated spoons with the melted white baking bar. Drizzle remaining melted bittersweet chocolate on white baking bar-coated spoons.

4 Refrigerate spoons for 30 minutes to allow chocolate to set up. Wrap each spoon separately and store in cool, dry place for 2 to 3 weeks. Makes 20 to 24 chocolate-covered spoons.

Fill the cup with the beans. Place on the saucer. Place a pair of chocolate spoons on top of the cup. Arrange tasseled cord around the base of the cup. Wrap extra spoons in cellophane bags; tie with gold ribbon.

also try this...

Wrap cellophane packages of spoons with gold curling ribbon to add even more cheer.

To present this gift you will need:
Matching teacup and saucer
Coffee beans
Gold-tasseled cord
Cellophane bags
Thin gold ribbon

christmas stars

Be the star of the party! Pickled star-shape fruits, presented in star-theme packaging, will provide hosts with a delicious holiday addition to their appetizer spread.

TO MAKE THE RECIPE...

pickled carambola

In some regions, carambola is sold by the name of star fruit. Choose fruit that is shiny and firm; allow it to ripen at room temperature until yellow-orange in color.

3 cups water
3 tablespoons salt
4 medium carambola
   (star fruit) (10 ounces
   total or 2½ cups),
   sliced ⅜ inch thick
1 cup sugar
½ cup white vinegar
½ cup water
4 inches stick cinnamon
½ teaspoon whole
   cloves
1 tablespoon finely
   shredded orange peel

1 In a large glass or ceramic bowl combine the 3 cups water and the salt. Stir in carambola. Allow to stand at room temperature for 4 hours or overnight. Drain in colander and rinse under cold running water for 3 minutes. Drain well. Return to bowl.

2 For syrup, in a medium saucepan combine sugar, vinegar, the ½ cup water, the cinnamon, and cloves. Bring to boiling, stirring to dissolve sugar; reduce heat. Simmer sugar mixture, uncovered, for 7 minutes.

3 Using slotted spoon, remove spices from syrup; discard. Add orange peel to syrup in saucepan. Pour syrup over carambola in bowl. Cool to room temperature.

4 Ladle into hot clean screw-top jars or a storage container. Cover and store in the refrigerator for at least 4 hours before using, or for up to 2 weeks. Makes about 2 cups pickles.

TO PRESENT THIS GIFT...

Fill bowl with carambola; replace lid. Using ribbon, tie up the dish as if it were a gift. Cut a 16-inch length of wire. String bugle beads and star buttons or beads on wire. Bend the ends to secure the beads. Wrap the beaded wire around the knob on the lid.

also try this...

For an alternative to star-shape beads, use inexpensive earrings for a special effect.

To present this gift you will need:
Sugar bowl with lid
Sheer ribbon
Wire cutter
Medium-weight craft
   wire
Bugle beads
Small star-shape
   buttons or beads

The hosts will love you for brightening their holiday table with this festively dressed, sprightly spread.

merry marmalade

red onion marmalade

 3 **large red onions, halved and thinly sliced (5 to 6 cups)**
 1 **tablespoon grated fresh ginger**
 2 **large cloves garlic, crushed**
 2 **cups packed light brown sugar**
 1 **cup cider vinegar**
 1 **cup red wine vinegar**

For a match made in heaven, introduce this spread to Christmas ham or turkey. Or serve it on the appetizer tray alongside cream cheese and crackers.

1 In a 4-quart Dutch oven or kettle combine all ingredients. Cook over medium heat to boiling. Reduce heat. Simmer, uncovered, for 30 to 40 minutes or until mixture is very thick and onions are very tender. Transfer to a bowl. Cover and store in the refrigerator for up to 4 weeks. Makes about 2 cups.

To present this gift you will need:
Glass jar
Scissors
Thin decorative paper or vellum
Curling ribbon
Medium-weight white paper
Pinking shears
Decorative paper in desired colors
Glue stick
Paper punch

TO PRESENT THIS GIFT... Fill the glass jar with marmalade. Cut a circle of decorative paper approximately 2 inches larger than the jar circumference. Cut the circle into a coil. Wrap around the jar. Tie generous lengths of curling ribbon around the jar handle. Curl the ends with scissors.

For the tag, cut a small rectangle from paper. Use pinking shears to cut a frame shape smaller than rectangle from decorative paper. Glue to rectangle. Let dry. Repeat with another color. Let dry. Punch a hole in one corner. Thread curling ribbon through hole.

also try this...
Cut coil from colored foil paper for an extra-festive effect.

No time to bake?
No problem! These cookie sandwiches, made completely from convenience items, stack up to one sweet and easy treat!

stack of sweetness

TO MAKE THE RECIPE...

chocolate-peppermint sandwiches

This is a perfect way to introduce kids to the pleasures of homemade gift-giving.

½ cup canned vanilla or chocolate frosting
 Red and/or green paste food coloring (optional)
3 tablespoons finely crushed striped round peppermint candies
44 chocolate wafers

1 In a small mixing bowl stir together frosting, food coloring (if desired), and crushed candies. Spread 1 level teaspoon frosting mixture each on flat side of 22 of the chocolate wafers. Top with the remaining chocolate wafers, flat side toward frosting mixture. Roll edges of cookie sandwiches in additional crushed candies, if desired. Store cookies in airtight container in the refrigerator for up to 3 days. Makes 22 cookie sandwiches.

TO PRESENT THIS GIFT... Stack three or four sandwiches and place in dish. Tie stack with ribbon to secure. Trim ribbon ends, if desired.

also try this...
Place a small candy cane in the ribbon while tying the bow.

To present this gift you will need:
Round shallow dish
Ribbon
Scissors

Milk Chocolate and Caramel
Clusters, page 209

between friends & neighbors

ween friends & neighbors between frienc

celebration in a bag

Start a party wherever you go! **Just bring along this bag of shortbread goodies, complete with a luscious lemon dipping sauce.**

macadamia nut shortbread

1¼ cups all-purpose flour
3 tablespoons brown sugar
½ cup butter
2 tablespoons finely chopped macadamia nuts
Powdered sugar (optional)
Purchased lemon curd or homemade Luscious Lemon Curd (see recipe, page 95)

The much-loved English goodie just got better—and richer—with a sprinkling of buttery macadamia nuts. When served alongside a little lemon curd, the classic cookie becomes a luscious dessert.

1 In a medium mixing bowl stir together flour and brown sugar. Using a pastry blender, cut in butter until mixture resembles fine crumbs and starts to cling. Stir in macadamia nuts. Form mixture into a ball and knead until smooth.

2 Pat or roll dough on a lightly floured surface into an 11¼×6-inch rectangle. Using a crinkle cutter, if desired, cut into 3×¾-inch or 2¼×¾-inch strips. Place strips about 1 inch apart on an ungreased cookie sheet.

3 Bake in a 325° oven about 10 minutes or until bottoms just start to brown. Transfer to wire racks to cool. Store in a tightly covered container at room temperature for up to 3 days or in the freezer for up to 3 months.

4 To serve, sift powdered sugar lightly over cookies, if desired. Serve cookies alongside lemon curd for dipping. Makes 30 to 40 cookies.

Trim the top of the bag with the pinking shears. Fill bag with shredded paper and shortbread. Fill plastic container with lemon curd. Place stickers on the bag and on the container lid. Loosely tie ribbon around bag.

also try this...

Use a delicate ribbon barrette to seal the bag.

To present this gift you will need:
White paper bag
Pinking shears
Shredded paper
Small plastic container with lid
Gold star stickers
Thin gold ribbon

a bucket
of bliss

As joyful as a day at the beach, **and just as easy,**
this pretty hand-decorated pail overflows
with mouthwatering candy.

almond-butter crunch

1 cup slivered almonds
½ cup butter
½ cup sugar
1 tablespoon light-
  colored corn syrup

If it's ease you're after, you've come to the right recipe. This candy delivers superb taste with just four ingredients and three simple steps.

1 Line bottom and sides of a 9-inch round baking pan (do not use a glass baking dish) with foil. Butter the foil heavily. Set pan aside.

2 In a 10-inch skillet combine almonds, butter, sugar, and corn syrup. Cook over medium heat until sugar is melted and mixture turns golden brown, stirring constantly (about 10 minutes).

3 Quickly spread mixture in the prepared pan. Cool about 15 minutes or until firm. Remove candy by lifting edges of foil. Peel off foil. Cool. Break candy into pieces. Store in a tightly covered container in a cool, dry place for up to 1 week. Makes ¾ pound candy.

TO PRESENT THIS GIFT... To make stripes on the pail, place several rubber bands around the pail. You can group the rubber bands or put them on randomly. To make the bow, wrap a rubber band around 6 to 8 bands. Attach the rubber band bow to the handle of the pail.

also try this...

Use colored string to decorate the pail, knotting the ends as needed.

**To present
this gift you
will need:**
Colored metal pail
Colored rubber bands

butter & bows

A shining cupful of apricot butter sits atop a glass snack tray that's reminiscent of church-basement socials— and just as warm and inviting.

apricot butter

3 tablespoons snipped dried apricots
½ cup butter or margarine, slightly softened
2 teaspoons sugar
1½ teaspoons grated fresh ginger or ½ teaspoon ground ginger

This sweet fruit butter goes great with muffins or tea breads. To prove it, present the spread alongside such baked treats.

1 In a small bowl place snipped dried apricots. Pour boiling water over apricots to cover. Let stand 5 minutes. Drain well.

2 In a small mixing bowl combine softened butter, sugar, drained apricots, and ginger. Beat until light and fluffy. Cover and chill until mixture begins to firm up, stirring once or twice. Serve immediately or cover and store in the refrigerator for up to 1 week. If made ahead, let stand at room temperature for 15 to 30 minutes before serving. Makes ¾ cup butter.

Place the butter in the cup. Wrap a ribbon around the cup, and tie into a bow by the cup handle. Trim the ribbon ends. Place the cup on the tray.

also try this...

Tuck a fresh herb sprig into the ribbon bow.

To present this gift you will need:
Clear glass snack tray with cup
Ribbon
Scissors

neighborly nibbles

Marinated chunks of tangy feta cheese—tucked into a leaf-wrapped flowerpot—make a sprightly surprise for a favorite neighbor.

marinated feta

2 tablespoons olive oil
2 tablespoons assorted snipped fresh herbs, such as dillweed, thyme, basil, oregano, and/or parsley
2 cloves garlic, minced
1 tablespoon lemon juice
1 teaspoon dried whole mixed peppercorns, cracked
½ teaspoon poppy seed
8 ounces feta cheese, cubed

Yes, you can buy cheese spreads at the grocery store, but you can't beat the fresh flavor found in this homemade version.

1 In a small bowl combine the olive oil, herbs, garlic, lemon juice, cracked peppercorns, and poppy seed. Stir until well mixed. Add cheese cubes and toss very gently to coat. Divide the mixture between two clean half-pint jars with lids.

2 Cover and store in the refrigerator for 3 to 5 days. To use, let stand at room temperature for 30 minutes before serving. Serve feta cubes on an appetizer tray. Makes 2 half-pint jars.

Feta spread: Prepare as directed above, except to serve, mash the cubes with the marinade and use as a spread on bread and crackers.

TO PRESENT THIS GIFT... Make sure the bowl fits nicely inside the flowerpot. Arrange leaves on the outside of the flowerpot. Hot-glue in place. Let glue dry. Tie ribbon around the leaves. Trim the ribbon ends, if desired. Fill bowl with feta cheese cubes (or spread).

also try this...
Use small bunches of dried flowers to trim the flowerpot.

To present this gift you will need:
Small glass bowl
Terra-cotta flowerpot
Silk leaves
Hot-glue gun and hot-glue sticks
Ribbon
Scissors

a basket of
bread & cheer

The bread basket just got more interesting.
Surround a dill and cheese loaf with a gauzy napkin and top it with an edible bloom.

dill and cheese beer bread

3 cups self-rising flour*
½ cup shredded cheddar cheese (2 ounces)
½ cup shredded Monterey Jack cheese with jalapeño peppers (2 ounces)
2 tablespoons sugar
1 tablespoon dillseed
1 teaspoon dried dillweed
1 12-ounce can beer

Forget rising, kneading, punching, and all that. You don't have to be an experienced bread baker to make this savory loaf. It's as simple as stirring and baking!

1 Grease the bottom and ½ inch up the sides of a 9×5×3-inch loaf pan; set aside.

2 In a large mixing bowl stir together the flour, cheddar cheese, Monterey Jack cheese, sugar, dillseed, and dillweed. Add beer and stir until well combined. Spread batter in the prepared pan.

3 Bake in a 350° oven about 45 minutes or until bread sounds hollow when lightly tapped. Cool in pan on a wire rack for 10 minutes. Remove bread from pan. Cool completely on wire rack. Serve or wrap and store in the refrigerator for up to 3 days. Makes 1 loaf (16 servings).

*Note: If desired, substitute 3 cups all-purpose flour plus 1 tablespoon baking powder, 1 teaspoon salt, and ¾ teaspoon baking soda for the self-rising flour.

TO PRESENT THIS GIFT... Line basket with napkin. Nestle loaf in napkin. Tie a yellow ribbon around the basket, then tie it into a bow on the top. Trim ends, if needed. Tuck an edible flower into the bow.

also try this...

For a more earthy presentation, use a natural basket and plaid ribbon, and tuck in a small fresh pepper.

To present this gift you will need:
Clean napkin in desired color
Elegant wire basket
Yellow ribbon
Scissors
Edible flower

timeless treat

What could be prettier than this citrus-peel treat sparkling in a cut-glass candy dish? It's an old-fashioned gift that's perfect for an old-time friend.

2 medium oranges
1⅓ cups sugar
⅓ cup water
Sugar

candied orange peel

While you're at it, prepare an extra batch of this recipe to keep on hand for garnishing cakes and cookies. It freezes well for up to 6 months.

1 Cut peels of oranges lengthwise into quarters, cutting just through the pulp to the surface of the fruit. Pry back the quartered peel using the back of a spoon. Using the bowl of the spoon, scrape away the pith (the soft, white part inside the peel). If white pith is left on, the peel will be bitter. Cut peel into ⅜-inch-wide strips. Wrap and refrigerate peeled fruit for another use.

2 In a 2-quart saucepan combine the 1⅓ cups sugar and the water. Cover and bring to boiling. Add orange peel strips. Return to boiling, stirring constantly to dissolve sugar. Reduce heat. Cook, uncovered, over medium-low heat. Mixture should boil at a moderate, steady rate over entire surface. Cook, stirring occasionally, for 15 minutes or until peel is almost translucent. Remove from heat.

3 Using a slotted spoon, remove peel from syrup, allowing each spoonful to drain over the saucepan about 30 seconds. Transfer peel to a wire rack set over waxed paper. Set cooked peel aside until cool enough to handle but still warm and slightly sticky. Roll peel in additional sugar to coat. Continue drying on the rack for 1 to 2 hours. Store, tightly covered, in a cool, dry place for up to 1 week or in the freezer for up to 6 months. Makes about 2 cups peel.

Begin wrapping cotton embroidery floss around the stem of the dish, gluing as you go and leaving a long tail free. Continue wrapping the stem until covered. Tie the floss ends into a bow. Trim the floss ends, if needed. Let glue dry.

also try this...

Use colorful chenille stems to wrap the stem of the dish.

To present this gift you will need:
1 skein orange-and-yellow variegated cotton embroidery floss
Small cut glass candy dish
Thick white crafts glue
Scissors

brown bagging
in style!

The saying "brown bagging it" takes on a whole new meaning when you beautify the vessel with stencils and ribbon, and tuck some spicy cookies inside!

giant ginger cookies

4½ cups all-purpose flour
4 teaspoons ground ginger
2 teaspoons baking soda
1½ teaspoons ground cinnamon
1 teaspoon ground cloves
¼ teaspoon salt
1½ cups shortening
2 cups granulated sugar
2 eggs
½ cup molasses
¾ cup coarse sugar or granulated sugar

Chewy and delicious, these cookies are giants in both size and snappy ginger flavor. They're the perfect ending to a brown-bag lunch.

1 In a medium mixing bowl stir together flour, ginger, baking soda, cinnamon, cloves, and salt; set aside.

2 In a large mixing bowl beat shortening with an electric mixer on low speed for 30 seconds to soften. Gradually add the 2 cups granulated sugar. Beat until combined, scraping sides of bowl occasionally. Beat in eggs and molasses. Beat in as much of the flour mixture as you can with the mixer. Using a wooden spoon, stir in any remaining flour mixture.

3 Shape dough into 2-inch balls using ¼ cup dough. Roll balls in the ¾ cup coarse or granulated sugar. Place about 2½ inches apart on an ungreased cookie sheet.

4 Bake in a 350° oven for 12 to 14 minutes or until cookies are light brown and puffed. (Do not overbake or cookies will not be chewy.) Cool on cookie sheet for 2 minutes. Transfer cookies to a wire rack to cool. Store in a tightly covered container at room temperature for up to 3 days or in the freezer for up to 3 months. Makes twenty-five 4-inch cookies.

Stamp the bag as desired. Let the ink dry. Carefully roll down the top of the bag. Using a crafts knife, cut two slits wide enough to accommodate the ribbon on each side of the bag top. Thread the ribbon up through a slit on one side of the bag, then across the top and down through another slit on the other side of the bag. Bring the other end of the ribbon under the bag and staple or glue the ends together. Let glue dry. Repeat for the second ribbon. Line bag with parchment paper or waxed paper.

also try this...

Use permanent markers instead of stamps to draw designs on the paper bag.

To present this gift you will need:
Stamp pad and stamp
Brown paper bag
Crafts knife
2 yards of wire-edge ribbon cut into 1-yard lengths
Stapler or thick white crafts glue
Parchment paper or waxed paper

nice nibbles

A retro container once used to hold leftovers now makes a stylish carrier for these irresistible, easy-to-tote snacks.

1   8-ounce thin baguette
½   cup butter or margarine
1   tablespoon snipped fresh basil or ½ teaspoon dried basil, crushed
⅛   teaspoon garlic powder

herbed crouton sticks

These king-size croutons make terrific dunkers for soups or dips and a fine accompaniment to salads.

1 Cut baguette in half horizontally. Cut bread into strips 3½ inches long by 1 inch wide (or a length that will fit into gift container); set aside. In a 12-inch skillet melt butter or margarine. Stir in basil and garlic powder. Add half the crouton sticks, stirring until coated with butter mixture. Arrange crouton sticks in a single layer in a shallow baking pan. Repeat with remaining crouton sticks.

2 Bake, uncovered, in a 300° oven for 25 to 30 minutes or until crouton sticks are dry and crisp, turning once. Cool completely. Store, tightly covered, at room temperature for up to 3 days or in the freezer for up to 3 months. Makes about 24 sticks.

TO PRESENT THIS GIFT... First arrange the crouton sticks in the container. Put the lid on to keep the sticks airtight. Wrap the container with a napkin or tea towel.

also try this...

If you do not have a lid for the container, place the sticks upright, cover with colored cellophane, and wrap with a kitchen towel.

To present this gift you will need:
Antique refrigerator dish from the '40s or '50s, or another brightly colored vintage container
Clean vintage tea towel or fabric napkin

pesto with a twist

A beaded jar plus **an out-of-the-ordinary version of pesto equals a delightfully bead-azzling gift for food lovers.**

spinach, sorrel, and orange pesto

¼ cup slivered almonds, toasted

1½ cups loosely packed fresh spinach leaves

1½ cups loosely packed fresh sorrel, arugula, or watercress leaves

⅓ cup olive oil

⅓ cup grated Parmesan or Romano cheese

½ teaspoon finely shredded orange peel

3 tablespoons orange juice

¼ teaspoon ground red pepper

⅛ teaspoon salt

It's amazing what you can do with pesto! Serve it as a condiment for sandwiches or grilled meats, swirl it into soups and dips, or use it in the most tried-and-true way: tossed with pasta for a fresh-and-simple main or side dish.

1 Place almonds in a food processor bowl or blender container. Cover and process or blend the almonds until finely chopped. Add the spinach and sorrel, arugula, or watercress; cover. With the machine running, gradually add the oil in a thin, steady stream, processing until the mixture is combined and slightly chunky. Add Parmesan or Romano cheese, orange peel, orange juice, ground red pepper, and salt. Process or blend just until combined.

2 To store, divide pesto into ¼-cup portions and place in airtight containers. Store in the refrigerator for up to 1 week or in the freezer for up to 3 months. To serve, bring pesto to room temperature. Makes ¾ cup pesto.

Wash and dry the jar. Avoid touching areas to be painted. To paint white dots, dip the handle end of the paintbrush into paint. Dot onto the raised dots or in rows as desired. Let the paint dry. To add smaller dots, dip the end of a toothpick into the desired colors of paint and dot in the middle of the white dots. Let dry. Bake the painted glassware in oven if instructed by the paint manufacturer. Let cool.

Cut a length of wire 8 inches longer than the neck circumference of the jar. Wrap 1 inch of one end of the wire around the handle of the paintbrush. Slip off brush. Thread colored beads on the wire alternating with white beads. Leave 2 inches without beads. Wrap the remaining end of wire around the paintbrush handle. Remove brush. Place the beaded wire around the neck of the jar. Twist the wire to secure. Twist the wire ends together.

also try this...

Use elastic thread instead of wire to make a bracelet for the jar trim.

To present this gift you will need:
Glass jar with or without raised dots
Glass paints in white and desired colors
Paintbrush
Round toothpick
White plastic-coated crafting wire
Large seed beads in white and desired colors

vinegar
vessels

The gourmet in your life **will discover many ways to use a gift of flavored vinegar. This one comes in an arty bottle topped with whimsical filagree.**

herbed vinegar

½ cup tightly packed fresh tarragon, thyme, mint, rosemary, or basil leaves
2 cups white wine vinegar
Fresh herb sprig (optional)

Plan ahead. The vinegar needs to stand for at least 2 weeks before using.

1 Wash desired herbs and pat dry with paper towels. In a small stainless-steel or enamel saucepan combine the herbs and vinegar. Bring almost to boiling. Remove from heat and cover loosely with 100-percent-cotton cheesecloth; cool. Pour mixture into a clean 1-quart jar. Cover jar tightly with a nonmetallic lid (or cover the jar with plastic wrap and tightly seal with a metal lid). Let stand in a cool, dark place for 2 weeks.

2 Line a colander with several layers of 100-percent-cotton cheesecloth. Pour vinegar mixture through the colander and let it drain into a bowl. Discard herbs.

3 Transfer strained vinegar to a clean 1½-pint jar or bottle. If desired, add a sprig of fresh herb to the jar. Cover jar with a nonmetallic lid (or cover with plastic wrap and tightly seal with a metal lid). Store vinegar in a cool, dark place for up to 6 months. Makes about 2 cups.

Cut a 6-inch piece of solder for the cork trim and an 18-inch piece for the neck of the bottle. On the short piece of solder, coil one end using needlenose pliers to start the coil. Coil both ends of the long piece of solder, leaving the center uncoiled. Wrap the long piece of solder around the neck of the bottle, arranging the end coils as shown. Use an ice pick to poke a hole in the center of the cork. Glue the straight end of the short solder piece in the hole. Let the glue dry.

also try this...
Thread a few silver beads or springs on the solder before coiling.

To present this gift you will need:
Wire cutters
Lead-free solder on a spool
Needlenose pliers
Bottle with cork
Ice pick
Silicone glue

a crate of
crackers

Heading to a party? Bring along a batch of homemade crackers cleverly stacked in a crate for a gift that can be enjoyed now or later.

TO MAKE THE RECIPE...

cumin-caraway rounds

- ³⁄₄ cup all-purpose flour
- ³⁄₄ cup rye flour
- 1 tablespoon caraway seed
- ½ teaspoon baking powder
- ½ teaspoon salt
- ½ teaspoon ground cumin
- ¼ teaspoon ground coriander
- ¼ cup butter, cut into 4 pieces
- ⅓ cup milk
- 1 egg white, beaten

These crispy crackers with caraway seed taste like rye bread with a crunch!

1 In a food processor bowl combine all-purpose flour, rye flour, caraway seed, baking powder, salt, cumin, and coriander. Add butter; cover and process until blended. Add milk and process just until mixture forms a dough (if necessary, add an additional 1 tablespoon milk).

2 Transfer dough to a floured surface and let stand 5 minutes. Roll to ⅛-inch thickness, and cut with a 2-inch cutter or use a knife to cut into desired shapes. Transfer cutouts to an ungreased baking sheet. Brush lightly with egg white. Using a fork, prick crackers all over.

3 Bake in a 350° oven for 15 to 17 minutes or until crisp. Cool completely on wire racks. Store in a tightly covered container in the refrigerator for up to 1 week or in the freezer for up to 1 month. Makes 40 crackers.

TO PRESENT THIS GIFT...

Place the crackers in the baskets, making sure a couple stack above top of each basket. Tie twine or ribbon around each basket and stacked crackers. Tie a bow at the top. Trim the twine or ribbon ends, if needed.

also try this...

If using woven baskets such as those shown, paint every other square to enhance the checkerboard design. Line baskets with parchment paper or waxed paper.

To present this gift you will need:
Small baskets
Twine or ribbon
Scissors

inspired spices

To Wendy

A few Caribbean-inspired strokes of the paintbrush **top off** the lively gift inside: a jazzy Jamaican rub for grilled chicken.

TO MAKE THE RECIPE...

2 tablespoons sugar
4½ teaspoons onion powder
4½ teaspoons dried thyme, crushed
1 tablespoon ground allspice
1 tablespoon ground black pepper
1½ to 3 teaspoons ground red pepper
1½ teaspoons salt
¾ teaspoon ground nutmeg
¼ teaspoon ground cloves

jamaican jerk rub

Ground pepper and spices give this rub a Caribbean kick. Just rub it on chicken before grilling for a lively dish that's easy as a tropical breeze!

1 In a small mixing bowl stir together the sugar, onion powder, thyme, allspice, black pepper, red pepper, salt, nutmeg, and cloves.

2 Transfer mixture to a small airtight container or bag. Store at room temperature for up to 6 months. Makes about ½ cup seasoning.

TO PRESENT THIS GIFT...

Wash and dry the shaker. Avoid touching the areas to be painted. With a paint marker, draw a zigzag line around the edge of the jar lid, adding dots as desired. Add another line in a contrasting color. Let dry. Include preparation directions, below, with gift.

For the tag, cut a small square from corrugated paper. Cut a smaller square from white card stock. Glue the white square in the center of the corrugated paper square. Let glue dry. Punch a hole in one corner. Thread cord through hole and tie onto shaker handle.

also try this...

Glue brightly colored buttons on the edge of the lid using a hot-glue gun and glue sticks.

PREPARATION DIRECTIONS

To use, sprinkle some of the mixture evenly over chicken and rub in with your fingers before grilling.

To present this gift you will need:

Plastic shaker jar with plastic cap
Paint markers in desired colors
Scissors
Corrugated paper
White card stock
Glue stick
Paper punch
Cord

charming carrots

A jar of picked carrots **suits up with a fringed collar that's playfully trimmed with rickrack.**

asian pickled carrots

1 16-ounce package peeled baby carrots
1 teaspoon salt
¼ cup peeled and julienned fresh ginger
3 whole allspice
¾ cup water
¾ cup rice vinegar
⅓ cup packed brown sugar
4 whole cloves
4 whole peppercorns

Packaged baby carrots make it convenient to create this gift. Served alongside imported meats and cheeses, the carrots add color and crunch to an appetizer spread.

1 In a saucepan cook carrots and salt, covered, in a small amount of boiling water for 3 minutes or until crisp-tender. Drain and place in 3 clean half-pint jars. Place some of the ginger and one whole allspice in each jar.

2 In a medium saucepan combine water, vinegar, brown sugar, cloves, and peppercorns. Bring mixture to boiling; reduce heat. Simmer, uncovered, for 5 minutes. Pour over carrots, ginger, and allspice in jars. Seal jars and store in the refrigerator for up to 3 months. Makes 3 half-pints pickled carrots.

TO PRESENT THIS GIFT... Trace around the lid onto the paper. Cut out slightly smaller than traced line. Place paper on lid, under the ring. Adjust ring on top of jar. Measure around the jar lid. From each tissue paper color, cut 1-inch-wide strips this length plus 1 inch. Fold each strip in half lengthwise. Cut fringes into folded edge from folded side, being careful not to cut strips in half. Glue the green strip to the bottom edge of the jar lid. Glue the yellow strip slightly above the green. Glue a piece of rickrack around the unclipped edge of the yellow strip. Let the glue dry.

For the tag, cut a rectangle from paper. Fold in half. Cut a smaller contrasting paper rectangle and glue to the tag front. Let glue dry. Punch a hole in the upper left corner. Thread ribbon through hole to tie onto jar.

also try this...

To trim the jar lid, use scraps of fabric, cloth braid, and fringe.

To present this gift you will need:
Decorative paper
Pencil
Scissors
Tape measure
Tissue paper in yellow and green
Thick white crafts glue
Orange rickrack
Colored paper
Paper punch
Orange ribbon

sweetness
and scones

The ultimate teatime treat rises to a new level **of extra-sweet with sprinklings of chocolate chips and coconut.**

TO MAKE THE RECIPE...

chocolate-coconut scones

If the recipient isn't a coconut lover, try the fruit scone version, below.

2 cups all-purpose flour
3 tablespoons sugar
2 teaspoons baking powder
¼ teaspoon salt
6 tablespoons butter
1 egg, beaten
½ cup purchased unsweetened coconut milk or milk
⅓ cup shredded coconut
⅓ cup miniature semisweet chocolate pieces
Milk (optional)
Coarse sugar (optional)

1 Lightly grease a baking sheet; set aside. In a medium mixing bowl combine flour, the 3 tablespoons sugar, the baking powder, and salt. Using a pastry blender, cut in butter until mixture resembles coarse crumbs. Make a well in the center of dry mixture; set aside.

2 In a small mixing bowl combine egg, coconut milk, coconut, and chocolate pieces. Add egg mixture all at once to flour mixture. Using a fork, stir just until moistened.

3 Turn dough out onto a lightly floured surface. Quickly knead by folding and gently pressing dough for 10 to 12 strokes or until dough is nearly smooth. On the prepared baking sheet, pat or lightly roll dough into a 7-inch circle. Cut into 8 wedges; do not separate wedges. If desired, brush tops of scones with milk and sprinkle with coarse sugar.

4 Bake in a 400° oven for 20 to 25 minutes or until golden. Transfer to a wire rack to cool for 5 minutes. Separate scones. Cool completely. Transfer to an airtight container or bag and store at room temperature for up to 3 days, or in the freezer for up to 3 months. Makes 8 scones.

Fruit Scones: Prepare scones as directed above except use milk instead of coconut milk, omit the coconut, and substitute ½ cup dried blueberries or currants, or snipped dried cherries, cranberries, or raisins, for the chocolate pieces.

TO PRESENT THIS GIFT...

Punch holes ½ inch in from the edge of the plate, making sure the holes are punched in sets, each set being 1 inch apart. Weave ribbon through the holes. Tie the ribbon ends into a bow. Trim the ribbon ends, if needed.

also try this...

Experiment with other weaving possibilities, such as shoelaces, cording, or braid.

To present this gift you will need:
Paper punch
Decorative paper plate
Ribbon
Scissors

breakfast
brightener

Welcome a new family into the neighborhood **with a ready-made breakfast granola piled inside a canister they can use over and again.**

TO MAKE THE RECIPE...

orange breakfast granola

House granolas are all the rage in hip breakfast spots, so your special homemade version will be quite the with-it gift. Eat it as you would breakfast cereal, or sprinkle it over ice cream or frozen yogurt for dessert.

- 3 cups regular rolled oats
- ½ cup toasted wheat germ
- ½ cup coarsely chopped hazelnuts (filberts) or sliced almonds
- ⅓ cup honey
- ½ teaspoon finely shredded orange peel
- ⅓ cup orange juice
- ½ teaspoon ground cinnamon
  Nonstick cooking spray
- 1 cup flaked or shredded coconut

1 In a large mixing bowl stir together the oats, wheat germ, and hazelnuts or almonds. In a small saucepan stir together the honey, orange peel and juice, and cinnamon. Heat just until boiling; remove from heat. Add honey mixture to oat mixture, tossing gently until coated.

2 Coat a 15×10×1-inch baking pan with nonstick cooking spray. Spread oat mixture evenly in pan. Bake in a 325° oven for 15 minutes. Add coconut to oat mixture and stir. Bake for 15 to 20 minutes more or until light brown, stirring once. Remove from oven and immediately turn out onto a large piece of foil; cool. Store in an airtight container at room temperature for up to 2 weeks or in the freezer for up to 3 months. Makes about 5 cups granola.

TO PRESENT THIS GIFT...

Cut a piece of ribbon to wrap around glass jar lid. Glue in place with crafts glue. Let dry. Hot-glue cinnamon sticks around the rim of the lid. Arrange and hot-glue wheat to the top of the lid. Hot-glue an artificial orange in the center of the lid. Let dry. Include preparation directions, below, with gift.

also try this...

Help keep the topper intact by spraying with a clear spray sealer.

To present this gift you will need:
Scissors
Ribbon
Clear jar
Thick white crafts glue
Hot-glue gun and hot-glue sticks
Cinnamon sticks
Wheat
Small artificial orange

PREPARATION DIRECTIONS

Spoon granola into a bowl. Top with any combination of fresh fruit, such as blueberries, sliced nectarines, blackberries, sliced strawberries, raspberries, and/or sliced, peeled peaches. Top with plain or vanilla yogurt or milk.

sweets for the sweet tooth

Pop by a friend's house with a treat you can indulge in together.
These clusters are great the day they're made,
and the recipient will cherish the pretty box
they came in for years to come.

milk chocolate and caramel clusters

12 vanilla caramels
½ cup milk chocolate pieces
2 tablespoons water
2 cups honey graham cereal, slightly crushed (about 1½ cups)
¾ cup peanuts

This treat comes together quickly, so it's great when you need a spur-of-the-moment gift. However, the candy will harden if allowed to sit too long, so give it—and encourage the recipient to enjoy it—the same day you make it. Tip: Work quickly when dropping the cookies onto the cookie sheets so the mixture doesn't harden in the saucepan.

1 In a heavy medium saucepan combine the caramels, milk chocolate pieces, and water. Stir over low heat until caramels are melted. Remove from heat. Stir in cereal and peanuts.

2 Working quickly, drop mixture from a teaspoon onto cookie sheets lined with waxed paper. Let stand until firm (about 30 minutes). Makes about 28 clusters.

Place a small amount of both paints on the plate. Do not mix. Paint the bottom of the box copper. While the paint is wet, use a fine paintbrush to paint in swirls and circles using dark brown. Let dry. Paint the lid dark brown. While the paint is wet, paint copper designs as done for the bottom of the box. Paint the edges of the lid copper. Let the paint dry. Line box and cover clusters with parchment paper or waxed paper to prevent food from coming into contact with painted surfaces.

also try this...

Check your crafts store for boxes in other shapes, such as stars, hexagons, and hearts.

To present this gift you will need:
Acrylic paints in dark brown and copper
Disposable paper plate
Paintbrush
Round cardboard box
Parchment paper or waxed paper

Color someone happy with this festive jar of bright, spicy-sweet spread.

snazzy spread

TO MAKE THE RECIPE... red pepper spread

4   7-ounce jars roasted
    sweet red peppers,
    drained
½   cup tomato paste
4   teaspoons sugar
1   teaspoon dried
    thyme, crushed
1   teaspoon salt
½   teaspoon garlic
    powder
⅛   teaspoon ground red
    pepper

Don't be mistaken! This red pepper spread is not for spicy-food lovers only. Here the main ingredient is the sweet red pepper, and it has been roasted for a mellow flavor. Garlic and ground red pepper (the spicy kind!) add just a little kick.

1 In a blender container or food processor bowl place sweet red peppers, tomato paste, sugar, thyme, salt, garlic powder, and ground red pepper. Cover and blend or process until nearly smooth. Cover and store in the refrigerator for up to 1 week. Serve with crackers or toasted baguette slices. Makes about 3 cups spread.

**To present
   this gift you
   will need:**
Glass jar
Paintbrush
Glass paints in black,
   white, purple,
   yellow, red, and
   light aqua

TO PRESENT THIS GIFT... Wash and dry the jar. Avoid touching the areas to be painted. Paint the lid black. Paint random black squares on the jar, each approximately 1 inch square. Let the paint dry. Mix a small amount of white with the purple paint to lighten it. Paint a large swirl on the jar lid. Paint small swirls over the squares on the jar using light purple, yellow, red, and light aqua. Let the paint dry. Bake the painted glassware in the oven if instructed by the paint manufacturer. Let cool.

also try this...

Use a silver metallic permanent marking pen to write "Red Pepper Spread" around the edge of the jar lid.

recipe index

craft index

sources

Beads are available at most arts, crafts, stitchery, and discount stores. For more information, contact:
Gay Bowles Sales/Mill Hill
P.O. Box 1060
Janesville, WI 53547
(www.millhill.com; or 800-356-9438)
Also contact:
Westrim Crafts
9667 Canoga Avenue
Chatsworth, CA 91311 or at
(www.westrimcrafts.com; 800-727-2727)
Another bead source:
Bodacious Beads
1942 S. River Road
Des Plaines, IL 60018
(847-699-7959)

Buttons are available at most fabric, crafts, and discount stores. For more information, contact:
JHB International, Inc.
1955 S. Quince Street
Denver, CO 80231
(www.buttons.com; 303-751-8100)

Chinese take-out containers are available at most paper goods and party supply stores. For more information, contact:
Papourri
1751 28th Street
West Des Moines, IA 50265
(515-223-7265)

Clay is available at most arts, crafts, and discount stores. For more information on Sculpey III clay, contact:
Polyform Products Co.
1901 Estes Avenue
Elk Grove Village, IL 60007
(www.sculpey.com; 847-427-0020)

For information on Crayola Model Magic, contact: www.crayola.com or 800-CRAYOLA

Decorative-edge scissors (also known as Paper Edgers) are available at most arts and crafts stores. For more information, contact:
Fiskars Consumer Products
305 South 84th Avenue South
Wausau, WI 54401
(www.fiskars.com; 800-950-0203)

Decorative papers are available at most arts stores. For more information, contact:
The Art Store
600 Martin Luther King Jr. Pkwy.
Des Moines, IA 50312
(www.shoptheartstore.com; 800-652-2225)

Decoupage Medium is available at most arts, crafts, and discount stores. For more information, contact:
Plaid Enterprises, Inc.
P.O. Box 2835
Norcross, GA 30091
(800-842-4197)

Embroidery floss is available at most stitchery, discount, and crafts stores. For more information, contact:
Coats & Clark
Consumer Services Dept.
P.O. Box 12229
Greenville, SC 29612-0229
Or contact:
DMC Corp.
10 Port Kearney, #E
Kearney, NJ 07032
Also contact: Herrschners at 800-441-0838

Flexible plastic cones are available at most crafts stores. To locate a Michaels arts and crafts store near you, contact: www.michaels.com

Leather lacing is available at most arts and crafts stores. To locate a Michaels arts and crafts store near you, contact: www.michaels.com

Paints are available at most arts and crafts stores. For more information, contact Plaid Enterprises, Inc.
P.O. Box 2835
Norcross, GA 30091
(800-842-4197)
Also contact:
DecoArt Paint
P.O. Box 386
Stanford, KY 40484
(800-367-3047)
For more information on glass paints, contact:
Delta Technical Coatings, Inc.
2550 Pellissier Place
Whittier, CA 90601
(800-423-4135)

Ribbons are available at fabric and crafts stores. For more information, contact:
C.M. Offray & Son, Inc.
Box 601, Route 24
Chester, NJ 07930
(908-879-4700)

Rubber bands are available at most arts and crafts stores. For more information, contact:
The Art Store
600 Martin Luther King Jr. Pkwy.
Des Moines, IA 50312
(www.shoptheartstore.com; 800-652-2225)

Thick white crafts glue is available at most arts, crafts, and discount stores. To locate a Michaels arts and crafts store near you, contact: www.michaels.com

Wire is available at most arts and crafts stores. For more information on metallic wire, contact:
Artistic Wire
752 Larch Ave.
Elmhurst, IL 60126
(www.artisticwire.com; 630-530-7567)
For more information on plastic-coated colored wire, contact: www.twisteez.com

metric cooking hints

By making a few conversions, cooks in Australia, Canada, and the United Kingdom can use the recipes in this book with confidence. The charts on this page provide a guide for converting measurements from the U.S. customary system, which is used throughout this book, to the imperial and metric systems. There also is a conversion table for oven temperatures to accommodate the differences in oven calibrations.

Product Differences

Most of the ingredients called for in the recipes in this book are available in English-speaking countries. However, some are known by different names. Here are some common U.S. American ingredients and their possible counterparts:
• Sugar is granulated or castor sugar.
• Powdered sugar is icing sugar.
• All-purpose flour is plain household flour or white flour. When self-rising flour is used in place of all-purpose flour in a recipe that calls for leavening, omit the leavening agent (baking soda or baking powder) and salt.
• Light-colored corn syrup is golden syrup.
• Cornstarch is cornflour.
• Baking soda is bicarbonate of soda.
• Vanilla is vanilla essence.
• Sweet green, red, or yellow peppers are capsicums.
• Golden raisins are sultanas.

Volume and Weight

U.S. Americans traditionally use cup measures for liquid and solid ingredients. The chart, below, shows the approximate imperial and metric equivalents. If you are accustomed to weighing solid ingredients, the following approximate equivalents will help.
• 1 cup butter, castor sugar, or rice = 8 ounces = about 230 grams
• 1 cup flour = 4 ounces = about 115 grams
• 1 cup icing sugar = 5 ounces = about 140 grams

Spoon measures are used for smaller amounts of ingredients. Although the size of the tablespoon varies slightly in different countries, for practical purposes and for recipes in this book, a straight substitution is all that's necessary.

Measurements made using cups or spoons always should be level unless stated otherwise.

EQUIVALENTS: U.S. = AUSTRALIA/U.K.

⅕ teaspoon = 1 ml
¼ teaspoon = 1.25 ml
½ teaspoon = 2.5 ml
1 teaspoon = 5 ml
1 tablespoon = 15 ml
1 fluid ounce = 30 ml
¼ cup = 60 ml
⅓ cup = 80 ml
½ cup = 120 ml
⅔ cup = 160 ml
¾ cup = 180 ml
1 cup = 240 ml
2 cups = 475 ml
1 quart = 1 liter
½ inch = 1.25 cm
1 inch = 2.5 cm

BAKING PAN SIZES

U.S.	Metric
8×1½-inch round baking pan	20×4-cm cake tin
9×1½-inch round baking pan	23×4-cm cake tin
11×7×1½-inch baking pan	28×18×4-cm baking tin
13×9×2-inch baking pan	32×23×5-cm baking tin
2-quart rectangular baking dish	28×18×4-cm baking tin
15×10×1-inch baking pan	38×25.5×2.5-cm baking tin (Swiss roll tin)
9-inch pie plate	22×4- or 23×4-cm pie plate
7- or 8-inch springform pan	18- or 20-cm springform or loose-bottom cake tin
9×5×3-inch loaf pan	23×13×8-cm or 2-pound narrow loaf tin or pâté tin
1½-quart casserole	1.5-liter casserole
2-quart casserole	2-liter casserole

OVEN TEMPERATURE SETTINGS

Fahrenheit Setting	Celsius Setting*	Gas Setting
300°F	150°C	Gas mark 2 (very low)
325°F	170°C	Gas mark 3 (low)
350°F	180°C	Gas mark 4 (moderate)
375°F	190°C	Gas mark 5 (moderately hot)
400°F	200°C	Gas mark 6 (hot)
425°F	220°C	Gas mark 7 (hot)
450°F	230°C	Gas mark 8 (very hot)
475°F	240°C	Gas mark 9 (very hot)
Broil		Grill

*Electric and gas ovens may be calibrated using Celsius. However, for an electric oven, increase the Celsius setting 10 to 20 degrees when cooking above 160°C. For convection or forced-air ovens (gas or electric), lower the temperature setting 10°C when cooking at all heat levels.